noodles ~~#2~~ 11?

Lasagna 121

chick peas 69

TASTE OF ERITREA

noodles
lasagna
chick peas
beer
sourdough
~~tartoni~~
ginger espuue

TASTE OF ERITREA

Recipes From One of East Africa's Most Interesting Little Countries

OLIVIA WARREN

HIPPOCRENE BOOKS, INC.
New York

ISBN 0-7818-0764-6

For information, address:
HIPPOCRENE BOOKS, INC.
171 Madison Avenue
New York, NY 10016

Printed in the United States of America.

TABLE OF CONTENTS

AN INTRODUCTION
TO ERITREA

Eritrea is a beautiful, small country in northeast Africa. It is on the area of the continent known as the Horn of Africa, with Ethiopia to the south, Sudan to the north and west, and the Red Sea as its eastern boundary. Eritrea won its independence from Ethiopia in 1991, after a long and bitter war.

Eritrea is a land saturated in optimism and determination. It is impossible to live in this country without being infected by the powerful conviction that here, anything is possible, anything at all. I am not sure where this attitude of confidence comes from, but it is as undeniable and obvious as the piercingly blue sky or the bright, benevolent sunshine. It is this national spirit pulsating through daily life that must always be kept in mind when considering Eritrea. It is a feature more difficult to pin down and explain than facts of language or topography, but it is a powerful, overwhelming force, and cannot be separated from any true understanding of the country.

The name Eritrea comes from an ancient Greek word for red, ερύθρος. It is the shade of red that Homer describes as the color of wine mixed with nectar, and a shade that Aeschylus calls the color of blood. It is the word used to describe the Red Sea, Ερύθρη θαλάσσα. Likening the Red Sea to wine or blood seems apt to me; having bathed in the waters of the Red Sea that caress Eritrea's eastern coast, I know that both poets are right in spirit, for these waters have both an intoxicating and vivifying effect.

Most of Eritrea may be classified as semiarid or desert. There is a small pocket of land with a tropical climate, but the majority of Eritrea is dry. The rains come twice a year, the "little rains" in April, and the "big rains" in July and August. Even during the rainy season, days dawn bright and clear in Asmara, the capital of Eritrea. However clouds gather every afternoon at about 3 o'clock, and the skies

1

open to send down a deluge of rain for about an hour, after which the clouds disperse and Asmara regains her perfect sunny skies.

Throughout Eritrea, the two most noticeable and ubiquitous types of uncultivated plant life are the cactus and the acacia tree. The cactus is the kind called a prickly pear in English. As it is not a plant that is native to Eritrea, it must have been imported at some time in the past, perhaps by the Italians as food for livestock. The Eritrean climate is ideal for it, and it is extremely prolific. One sees it everywhere, and there is some concern that it is out-competing many kinds of native plant life. However, it is an undeniably useful plant. Camels and oxen both eat it with relish, entirely untroubled by the sharp thorns. While I was in Eritrea, the government started a campaign to get people to think of the cactus pads as a human food source as well. It is thought that if drought and famine strike Eritrea, the population could survive on the cactus. The Eritrean television station had a program that showed how the thorns could be removed and how the pads could be cooked. Most Eritreans were shocked at the idea of eating what they consider animal fodder, and though I assured many people that cactus is often eaten in Mexico, the concept of eating cactus pads was considered a great joke.

However, every year, after the rainy season, the cacti produce a very popular fruit. Men and women pick the prickly pears using an empty tin can with a sharpened rim attached to the end of a very long pole. The harvester lifts the can up to where the fruit is attached to the cactus, and with a skillful twist of the wrist the prickly pear is cut from the plant and falls into the can. Prickly pears have a tough skin and many sharp spines, some of which seem invisible. The prickly pear sellers wear heavy gloves when they handle the fruit. They slice open the skin with a sharp knife, peel it back and the red flesh falls into a waiting bowl. The fruit is sweet, rather bland, and full of small edible seeds.

The acacia trees are another very prominent feature of the Eritrean landscape. The variety that is most common in Eritrea is rather small. The branches spread out like an umbrella, atop a thin straight trunk. The acacia is a very important source of food for animals, especially goats. One often sees goats standing on their hind legs, with forefeet braced against the tree trunks, contentedly nibbling. The goats don't seem to be troubled by the thorns on the trees as they eat the small, gray-green leaves.

What we now know as Eritrea was once an area of land with no definite borders. It was not definitively named until the nineteenth century. This area was a region with many influences. Much of the country lay within the Axumite Empire, an African empire that flourished from the third to the sixth century. With the decline of the Axumite Empire, the Turks had a great impact, especially along the coast of the Red Sea. In the port city of Massawa, that influence can still be seen in the architecture of the buildings and the dress and religion of the people, who are predominantly Muslim.

Massawa is a city on a series of islands in the Red Sea, connected by causeways, little wider than the width of a road. It is extremely pleasant to walk across these causeways and look down to observe the teeming life in the Red Sea. Some of these fish are very beautiful. Large angelfish are common, brilliantly colored with splashes of turquoise and violet. They glide about in the clear water like living objects d'art. I would often see children fishing there, by the side of the road. They seemed to be using nothing more than string and a piece of bread as they pulled in fish after fish.

The Turkish influence in Massawa is very visible. There is a large, blue-domed palace that was built for the Turkish governor. Later, it served as the Imperial Palace when the Ethiopian emperor was in Massawa. Like most of the buildings here, it was bombed in the war for independence. There is some talk of leaving it in ruins, with gaping holes in its roof, as a memorial to the horrors of the war.

Though heavily damaged by the war, one can still see evidence of the time when Massawa was a beautiful resort city, filled with hotels and villas as white and ornate as wedding cakes. There are labyrinthine streets winding past markets and wooden-roofed bazaars. Wooden lattice-enclosed balconies jut from houses. And of course there is the port. The port of Massawa is said to be the safest on the eastern side of the continent, and it bustles with both large and small ships.

In addition to the Turks, there were other influences on Eritrea. From the south, there was the encroachment of the Abyssinian kingdom. Though not always a cohesive entity, the landlocked

Abyssinian kingdom never stopped trying to gain a foothold in Eritrea, primarily to have access to the port at Massawa. The importance of this valuable port on the Red Sea cannot be overestimated. From ancient to modern times, Massawa has always been a major point of contention.

There were also European influences. The European colonial ventures in Africa during the nineteenth century have been aptly termed, "The Rush for Africa." In addition to the European colonizers, the more aggressive of the existing African nations tried to take parts of neighboring territory; in the first half of the nineteenth century, Egypt made strong attempts to gain Eritrea. The people then living in the area were not pleased at the prospect of being colonized by either the Egyptians or the Abyssinians. The several European powers that were making overtures were viewed as a lesser evil. The English established a consulate in Massawa in 1849, but were not interested in establishing a colony there. There were some French in Eritrea, but France established a stronger foothold further south in Djibouti. So it was the Italians who actually succeeded in colonizing Eritrea.

Italy joined the scramble for Africa late, having been caught up in her own unification efforts, so it wasn't until the 1880s that Italy was a strong enough entity to attempt colonization. After much intrigue, a few skirmishes, and one major battle with the Abyssinians, the Italians gained most of what is now Eritrea. They immediately set about improving and industrializing their new colony. In Asmara, the capital city, they installed water and sewage systems. Irrigation systems were built, roads were created, and Italian colonists came in droves.

The colonists were given land and they started planting cotton, vegetable crops, and orchards. There was also some industry, including a match company and biscuit factory. Salt was mined in Assab, and potash was mined in Denkalia. There were vineyards and wineries, the largest one owned by a man named Melotti.

In 1922 when fascism came to Italy, additional interest was focused on the colony in Eritrea. Italy poured money into even more improvements and many more colonists came. They built a railroad that twisted and climbed from Massawa to Asmara, a distance of 115 kilometers, that went from sea level to 8,000 feet above. The railroad continued across Eritrea to the town of Keren, and further to Agordat. They also built the longest aerial tramway in the world; it ran from the high plateau of Asmara down to the plains 8,000 feet below. This tram was mostly for freight, but I am told it took the occasional passenger, and the view, impressive even from the sharply twisting road, must have been incredible from a cable car.

This Italian-fueled boom lasted until World War II. In 1941 the British captured Eritrea and held it until the early 1950s. The British made a few changes in the infrastructure of Eritrean government, but to a large degree, it remained as it had been. One seemingly minor change had far-reaching effects. British soldiers wanted beer, and there was none in Eritrea. The Melotti winery agreed to brew beer if the British military governor would allow the importation of the ingredients. Melotti beer became extremely popular, first with the British, Italians, and Eritreans, and later with all the other foreign communities that flooded Asmara: Americans, Ethiopians, Israelis, Eastern Europeans, Cubans, and Russians. Even now, Melotti beer is ubiquitous in Eritrea.

Eritrea under the Italians had a largely state-subsidized economy, and this was not a practice that the British continued to any large extent. So the falsely buoyant economy began to deflate. By 1947 Eritrea had serious economic difficulties. Unemployment was high, and Eritrea was in the midst of a depression.

At this same time, a few years after the end of World War II, the world was deciding the fate of all former Italian colonies. It is here that the forces influencing the destiny of Eritrea become rather complex, and the foundations for thirty years of bitter war were laid. Most of the Eritreans themselves wanted independence. Many in the world community felt that Eritrea, in the middle of a depression and unused to independence for so long, was not ready to be simply a free nation. Therefore, some thought Eritrea should become a protectorship for ten years or so, and then allowed entire independence. Ethiopia, Eritrea's powerful southern neighbor, wanted Eritrea annexed and brought into the Ethiopian Empire under Emperor Haile Selassie. This was primarily so Ethiopia would gain Massawa, the important Red Sea port.

Even the Americans became involved in Eritrea. At this time, early in the Cold War, the United States began to have an interest in Eritrea, whose clear air and high plateau made it an ideal spot to establish a communications base. In 1950, with American encouragement, the United Nations determined that Eritrea would be federated to Ethiopia. Eritrea was supposed to be relatively self-governing, but Haile Selassie propelled Eritrea to become, more and more, like a northern province of Ethiopia. As international interest in Eritrea declined, Ethiopia took greater control. When Tigrinya, the main language of Eritrea, was outlawed, and only Amharic, the main language of Ethiopia, was taught in schools, Eritreans attempted to protest to the United Nations but were denied access. Older Eritreans tell of the time when Ethiopian soldiers came into Asmara, gathered up all the schoolbooks written in Tigrinya, took them to the edge of town, and burned them. Eritreans saw no way to end Ethiopian rule except by armed struggle. And so, in about 1960, a long and devastating conflict was born.

The struggle to liberate Eritrea from Ethiopian rule began as a mostly Muslim movement because Muslims were alarmed at the thought of domination by Ethiopia, a resolutely Christian country. These first fighters named themselves the Eritrean Liberation Front, the ELF, and their ideology was largely Marxist. Gradually, however, the movement for a free Eritrea became not a Muslim movement, nor a Christian one, but an *Eritrean* movement. At this time, in the mid-1960s, Ethiopia was having internal troubles of her own. Many Ethiopians were against the rule of Haile Selassie, and they too, were Marxist. There were uprisings against Haile Selassie, and mutinies in the army. Assailed in the north by Eritreans fighting for independence, and from within by Marxist revolutionaries, the Ethiopian government toppled. In September 1974, on the Ethiopian New Year's Day, Emperor Haile Selassie was deposed and placed under house arrest until his death in 1975. There was a great slaughter of aristocrats, and a communist government called the Dergue, with Mengistu Hailemariam as its leader, took power.

Ethiopia, which still controlled Eritrea, was now a communist country, and although Eritrea did not have independence, she had a communist government, and for some ELF fighters, that was enough.

However, many other Eritreans felt that the fight for freedom should go on. This caused a major split in the Eritrean freedom movement, and when the dust cleared, many of the communist members of the ELF had gone to Sudan, Europe, or Ethiopia. Those who remained were now less Marxist since they were now, after all, fighting the Marxist government of Ethiopia, and this group of fighters were now known as the EPLF, the Eritrean Peoples Liberation Front.

The Ethiopian army was well supplied with funds and weapons by the Soviet Union, which was happy to have a communist foothold in Africa. With the decline of the Soviet Union in the late 1980s, support of Ethiopia collapsed. This may have shifted the balance of power sufficiently to allow the Eritreans to defeat Ethiopia in May of 1991. Ethiopian President Mengistu Hailemariam fled taking, it is said, nothing but cartons of money. The Ethiopian troops occupying Asmara also fled, heading south towards Addis Ababa. The EPLF retook Asmara, the capital of Eritrea, and the war was over.

And so, after almost thirty years of fighting, the Eritreans were finally a victorious people in an independent country. The war has left great devastation behind it. Yet, despite the destruction caused by this terrible war, the feeling of joy and vigorous enthusiasm for the future is palpable throughout Eritrea.

Some good things have come out of the war. The first and perhaps most important thing is the tremendous feeling of unity among all Eritreans. Eritrea is a country with three religions, nine tribes, and several languages, yet I feel sure that internal strife will never be a problem for Eritrea, as it is for so many other African nations. Thirty years fighting a common enemy has given Eritreans such a feeling of brotherhood that I can't imagine any differences of culture will ever divide them. Interesting examples of setting aside differences abounded during the war. For instance, both the Eritrean Christians and Muslims have strict rules regarding the slaughter of animals for food. The animals must be killed in a particular way, with certain prayers recited. However, often both Muslims and Christians would be together fighting in the field. If they were lucky enough to find and kill an animal for food, the rigid rules of both religions were put aside, and the animal would be slaughtered with the single prayer, "Victory to the Martyrs!" (The Eritreans who died in the struggle for freedom are all known as Martyrs.) This problem, which could have led to great disharmony, instead became a unifying force.

This unity of country is tremendously important to the Eritrean government. They owe their victory over the Ethiopians, in the face of incredible odds, to this unity. Many things, some subtle and others obvious, are being done even now to maintain unity. For example, each of the ten provinces of Eritrea once had its own name. There were feelings of pride in one's own province, and hence some scorn felt for all other provinces. Ethiopia did what it could to nurture and inflame these feelings of antagonism between provinces during the war. In January of 1996 the Eritrean government eradicated these names, and now the provinces are known only by geographical designations: Central, Northern, Northeastern, Southern, and so on.

This is very characteristic of the new government. The new government has a president, Isaias Afewerki, who was a great hero in the war, and a parliament, mostly made up of notable war veterans. It is interesting to note that there are female members of parliament. Women always had a certain degree of power in Eritrea. They could own land in their own names and could obtain a divorce as easily as their husbands, for instance. But the war, in which a great many women fought alongside men, has further increased their sphere of responsibility and respect. The new government seems to be feeling its way along the road of independence carefully, and with great forethought. They seem to think deeply, and then act in a way that smoothes out any areas of possible future contention.

For the past several years the government has been working on a constitution, and they are slowly moving toward a true democracy. If pressed for a label, I would have to call the present government one of benevolent paternalism, and it seems to be working remarkably well. It really is appropriate that the government should be a kind of father figure to the people of a country who have such a tremendous family feeling for one another.

Family is immensely important to Eritreans. Even into old age, there are no more important people on earth than one's mother, father, sisters, and brothers. But the feelings of kinship extend beyond the boundaries of one's own personal family. In fact, it is common to address a person whose name you don't know by a familial term, "Sister," "Brother," "Grandmother," and so on. I'm sure Eritreans never gave it a thought, and were just translating their usual words straight into English, but I was always delighted to be called "Sister." This family closeness begins with physical closeness; babies are carried in pouches called *ma'hazel,* on their mother's backs until they can walk. These pouches are made of leather and are decorated with cowry shells and blue beads. A gauzy, white shawl known as a *shama* is thrown over the pouch and the baby and protects it from flies and dust.

The *shama* is also an important part of the traditional clothing for women. It is worn as a shawl with a dress that has a long skirt made of several layers of dazzling white diaphanous cotton. The dresses are embroidered around the neckline and down the front in a single column that ends near the hemline, usually in the form of a cross. The embroidery is dense, brightly colored, and very beautiful. The traditional clothing of the men consists of white shoes, white pants, and a white jacket. They usually carry a short white cane or a fly switch made from white horsehair.

The traditional hair style of the women is many rows of fine braids running back from the forehead, back over the crown of the skull, and then left loose to fluff out on the back of the head. Women commonly dye the palms of their hands with henna and married women dye the soles of their feet as well. Henna is sold in all the market places as a green powder. This is added to extremely hot water and the palms or soles are dipped into this mixture until an almost black color is achieved.

Ceremonial facial scars are often seen on both men and women. The most usual in Eritrea are two short parallel lines on each temple. Facial tattoos are also common. These are usually a blue cross on the forehead, or a blue necklace tattooed around the neck. The tattoos on the neck are thought to cure goiters. Many people, usually women, also have their gums tattooed. A thorn is used to puncture the flesh, and kohl (antimony sulfide) is used to pigment. Only the upper gum is tattooed, and the placement of the tattooing is significant. Unmarried people tattoo only the small area above the two front teeth and the areas above the first bicuspids, and married people have the entire upper gum tattooed. A blue-gummed smile is considered to be very beautiful. It certainly does make already eye-catching smiles even more noticeable.

It is interesting to note that most Eritreans have extraordinarily beautiful white teeth. It is likely that this has a great deal to do with genetics, and in some areas of Eritrea there may be some natural fluoridation of the drinking water, however, it is impossible to discount the importance of the *mo'its*. A *mo'its* is a twig from a particular kind of tree. I was told it was a variety of unfruiting olive tree. When one end of the twig is chewed it frays, and it is then rubbed along the teeth and gums. People carry a *mo'its* around all day and use it whenever their hands are not occupied with anything else. I, and all the travelers I met, quickly picked up this salubrious habit. It's a very pleasant sensation, but until you know the explanation it seems inexplicably odd that everyone, young and old, male and female, should have a stick in his mouth most of the time. The twigs are sold for a few cents and last for a few weeks of constant use. I met a traveler who found it an invaluable aid in his quest to quit smoking. He was sure he wouldn't be able to find these twigs in Germany, so before he returned home he astonished a young *mo'its* peddler by buying out his entire supply.

Life in Eritrea is very gregarious, and societal expectations in the area of social etiquette are exacting. One afternoon an Eritrean woman I knew asked if I would like to go with her to the charcoal merchant to buy charcoal. Of course I said yes, and as we wended our way quickly through Asmara I commented that I had never walked on these streets, as I usually used the main thoroughfares. My friend told me that we were using these little roads because if we walked on the avenues she would meet too many people that she knew and would have to stop and greet each one and we would *never* get to the charcoal yard before it closed.

When two Eritreans meet, they always greet each other in the same traditional way. They clasp hands and kiss each other's cheeks, first the right cheek, then the left, then the right. The kisses are interspersed with simultaneous queries about the well-being of the friend and his family. This simplified greeting only occurs when an Eritrean meets someone whom he sees often. When meeting after a long separation, the kissing goes on for a considerable time while inquiries are made after the health and happiness of even distant relations.

This feeling of family connection among Eritreans is apparent in countless other ways. Any adult feels it his right and obligation to correct the behavior of any child, whether he knows the child or not. And any child feels bound to respect the word of any adult as he would a parent. Perhaps this is common in other countries, perhaps this was even the case in America a few score years ago, but I found it so astonishing I wouldn't have believed it had I not seen it for myself.

I remember walking to the market one evening with an Eritrean friend when suddenly we heard a whistle and some music began to play. I didn't know what was happening. I looked around and saw that all the cars on the avenue had stopped where they were, and all the drivers had gotten out and were standing next to them. Everyone turned and faced toward a single point. I turned too, and saw that the Eritrean flag in front of a nearby government building was being lowered for the evening. Just then, a group of small children walked by, talking and laughing. My Eritrean friend briefly admonished them and they immediately stopped and solemnly turned to face the flag until the ceremony was over.

Perhaps it is this family feeling that accounts for the almost complete lack of crime. In all the time I was there I never experienced any offense, and I never heard of anything untoward happening to anyone else. Or perhaps this lack of crime comes from the strong feeling that after so many years of war and upheaval, tranquility must reign.

The seat of the new government is in Asmara. It is a city situated on an 8,000-foot-high plateau, and has what is perhaps the world's most perfect climate. The air is dry, no malarial mosquitoes venture to that altitude, the sun shines almost constantly, and the temperature ranges from 65° to 78°F. Asmara is a city laid out with care. It is extraordinarily clean; there is almost no rubbish on the ground. I couldn't understand how this was possible, since I had only seen one outdoor trash can in all of Asmara. It all became clear, however, one morning at dawn, when I saw an army of women in blue jackets sweeping up all the trash on the main streets. They are the widows of fighters who died during the war. The government pays them to clean the streets.

The main street, renamed Liberation Avenue after the war, is a broad boulevard lined with palm trees. At one end of Asmara, the avenue bends to become the road that leads to Massawa. All along Liberation Avenue are cafés and bars and shops. Near one end, there is the grand marquee of the Cinema Impero.

This enormous movie theater shows old, B-grade horror flicks. They are appallingly bad, but I never missed one. They were worthwhile simply for their novelty value, and for the luxury of hearing English spoken for a few hours. The projectionist played a short film before every movie. These were the most astounding collection of cinematic odds and ends that can be imagined. Some were newsreels from England in the 1960s, one was a short film about French skiing, another was about laying buoys in the English Channel. By far the most amazing short that I saw was an Italian newsreel filmed during World War II. It showed Mussolini strutting around, giving speeches, getting on trains, and shaking hands with Hitler. Patriotic music blared in the background and a man with a deep and rolling voice spoke words that were no doubt stirring to Italians during the war.

Outside the Cinema Impero, further along Liberation Avenue, is the Catholic cathedral. It was built, according to a plaque inside, in 1922, and Benito Mussolini is listed as one of its benefactors. This is a large, imposing structure, and its bell tower can be seen from most places in the city. The bell tower has 142 steps to the top, as I found out on my first day in Asmara when a young man in a blue smock ran up to me and asked if I would like to climb them. Naturally I did. All the wooden steps are rickety, some are missing altogether, and some have become the final resting places for a few unfortunate pigeons. However, after reaching the top, I was rewarded with the beautiful view of all Asmara stretching out beneath me.

At the far end of Liberation Avenue, the road ends when it intersects Avenue of the Martyrs. At this intersection is a very lovely outdoor café. It is not at all difficult to spend the day sitting here, writing postcards or reading, sipping coffee or fruit juice. Behind the café are broad terraced steps. At the top of them is the big white building that houses the President's office. A few hundred yards to the left are the gates of what was the Imperial Palace when Eritrea was under Ethiopian rule. For a few cents, you are admitted and are free to wander the grounds. This is perhaps the most beautiful garden in Eritrea, filled with bougainvillea, poinsettia bushes, palm trees, and fountains. It also houses three museums. In the old stables, there is the Ethnographic Museum, which displays objects used in traditional Eritrean life: baskets, swords, hippopotamus-hide shields, capes and dresses, platters, and rugs. In another outbuilding, is the Military Museum. It has a fascinating collection of the weapons that were used during the war for independence. There are machine guns and rocket launchers, rifles, cannons, tanks, and land mines. And in the beautiful yellow mansion that was once the palace, is the Archeological Museum which, as far as I could tell, is never open.

Within walking distance from here are the many restaurants and cafés filled with the food and drink that make spending time in Eritrea so enjoyable. In Asmara the Italian influence on food is most apparent. The Italians are responsible for the many cafés that are tucked here and there throughout Asmara. The Italians are also responsible for the whole concept of a café life in the city. The day's pace is slow enough to accommodate breaks to spend time in a café, sipping a cappuccino while enjoying a pastry and some pleasant conversation.

The Italians brought wonderful food to Eritrea: pasta, pastries, pizza, *fritatta, capretto, crème caramel* and *macedonia di frutta,*and many others. Although most of the Italians have left, these dishes live on, and many have acquired distinctly Eritrean modifications. And it is the Italians who brought the majority of the fruits and vegetables now eaten to Asmara. These fruits and vegetables are still commonly prepared the Italian way, but often their names have been altered slightly, changing as language does when left alone. For example, the word for tomato in Italian, *pomodoro*, has become *commoderé*.

The other cultures that have spent time in Eritrea have also left lasting impressions on the local food. It seems likely that it was the Turks who introduced chili peppers, and as a result, much of traditional Eritrean food is very spicy. The British were responsible for the brewing of European beer in Eritrea, and now beer is drunk as commonly as the native alcoholic drinks, *suwa* and *m'es*. And it must have been the Egyptians who brought the delicious and popular bean stew called *fül* to Eritrea.

The traditional food of Eritrea is similar in many ways to Ethiopian food. The staple carbohydrate is *ingera*, a large round pancake-like bread. It is made of teff, a very tiny gray grain, sorghum, or wheat flour. It is slightly sour, as its leavening comes from a fermentation process similar to that used to make sourdough bread. A common traditional dish eaten with *ingera* is *zigni*, a spicy stew made with either meat, chicken, fish, or vegetables. Also commonly eaten is *alicha*, another stew which is milder than *zigni* and is usually made with vegetables. *Tum'tumo* is a mild lentil dish, and *shiro* is a delicious spicy legume puree.

Many traditional Eritrean dishes are entirely vegetarian. There are about 150 "fasting" days for members of the Eritrean Orthodox Church, on which no animal products may be eaten. Neither members of the Eritrean Orthodox Church, nor any of the Muslim population eat pork. There are strict dietary rules for both Muslims and Christians and on the windows of butcher shops are large signs saying which practices are followed in that particular shop. Although I saw very few pork dishes while I was in Eritrea, it is possible to buy pork products like *pancetta* and salami, imported from Italy.

Eritrean food is usually served on a large tray. Several *ingera* cover the tray and one or more kinds of food are ladled onto this bread. The food is eaten communally. People sit around the tray on low seats. Before the meal, someone, usually the youngest member of the household, circulates around the tray with a basin of water and a towel, so hands may be washed. Everyone eats from the same tray, tearing off pieces of *ingera* and scooping up the food. There are no utensils and only the right hand may be used to eat. There is a knack to it, but it is not at all difficult. It is very common, as a gesture of affection, for one person to scoop up food and put it in another's mouth.

Eritrean hospitality is overwhelming. I was invited to eat in the homes of many people and this was always a rather stressful event, for it is not enough to eat simply to satiation. Rules of etiquette seem to demand that a guest eat until the point of pain. The first time I was invited to eat at an Eritrean's home, wishing to be polite, I began by eating whatever was in front of me. The food was marvelous, but I quickly realized that I would be eating all night if I didn't take some action. I said the food was delicious, but really, I was quite full. More food was put down and I was urged to eat. I politely took a few mouthfuls. Really, I said, it was wonderful, but I'd had enough. More food was put down, and I received disappointed looks until I ate some of it. This went on until, suffering intense discomfort, I abandoned all pretense of politeness and said, "No, no. Really, I can't eat any more." Far from being offended, my hosts simply laughed and ignored my protests, putting more food in front of me. And even by not picking up any food, I couldn't save myself, for some friendly soul would pick up some food and put it in my mouth. This was always done with the greatest good nature, and I'm sure no one ever realized how panicked I was at the prospect of one more mouthful. But even as I walked home, treading gently and bearing my acutely distended stomach before me, I had to admit that it really had been a delightful evening. Every time I was asked to dine at an Eritrean's house, I always accepted and every time, I left absolutely crammed to the gills with more food than I would have thought possible. There may actually be a way to refuse food and be taken seriously, but if there is, I never found it.

The following recipes encompass a wide range of foods and beverages that are found in Eritrea. Some are very simple, others are more complex. Many of these recipes are for traditional Eritrean dishes, while others are for foods that have been brought to Eritrea by the many cultures that have influenced this area. There are some recipes for purely Italian foods that were once commonly served in restaurants in Asmara, but which are now only to be found in the homes of the remaining Italians.

Preparing the following recipes and eating these foods will give you some idea of how delightful it is to spend time in Eritrea, a truly wonderful country.

Staple
Ingredients

🔳 RED PEPPER SPICE MIXTURE
(Berbere)

This is the most fundamental ingredient in Eritrean food. This recipe is not the way it is made in Eritrea. There, the red chili peppers are harvested and dried in the sun, as are the garlic bulbs. The spices are bought whole at the market. Each ingredient is prepared by a combination of drying, roasting, pounding, and grinding. Making this mixture in Eritrea is a long and tedious process which takes several days. However, *berbere* will keep for several months, or even longer if you add 6 tablespoons of oil. The spice paste you get by adding oil is called *da'lik* and may be used interchangeably with *berbere*.

    2 cups ground red pepper
    5 tablespoons garlic powder
    2 tablespoons onion powder
    2 tablespoons ground ginger
    2 tablespoons ground cloves
    2 tablespoons salt
    1 tablespoon ground cumin
    2 teaspoons ground fenugreek
    2 teaspoons cinnamon
    2 teaspoons ground cardamom
    1 teaspoon ground black pepper

YIELD: 3 CUPS

1. Combine all the ingredients. Mix thoroughly.
2. Store the spice mixture in an airtight container.

takes 3 days + 1 day later

❧ FLAT SOURDOUGH BREAD
(Ingera) *millet*

In Eritrea, this is usually made from a very small gray grain called teff. This recipe uses the ingredients and methods that Eritreans use to make *ingera* in America. This bread is an integral part of most traditional Eritrean meals. *Ingera* serves as both plate and utensil; foods are ladled onto it, and pieces are torn off and used to scoop up the food. It takes three days to prepare the sourdough starter and an additional day to make the bread.

2 cups all-purpose flour
8 cups self-rising flour
½ cup cornmeal
9 teaspoons solid shortening

YIELD: 18 ROUNDS

1. Mix the all-purpose flour with 2 cups of water. Put the mixture in a large jar and cover the jar with plastic wrap.
2. Let the jar stand at room temperature for 3 days. This is the sourdough starter. Discard the water that has risen to the top of the starter.
3. In a large bowl, mix together the self-rising flour, cornmeal, 8 cups of water, and all of the sourdough starter. Let this batter stand at room temperature for 24 hours. It will become bubbly.
4. Remove 1 cup of the batter to a pot and add ½ cup of water. Cook this mixture over a low heat while stirring until it becomes thick, about 10 minutes.
5. Remove the mixture from heat and let it cool. Stir the mixture back into the batter.
6. Add 2½ cups of water and mix well. Let the batter stand at room temperature for 2 hours.
7. Remove 3 cups of the batter and put it into the jar you used to make the sourdough starter. Refrigerate the batter and use it as the sourdough starter the next time you make *ingera* (beginning with step 3.)

8. Melt ½ teaspoon of the solid shortening in a large frying pan.
9. Remove 1 cup of the batter from the bowl and pour it in a stream into the hot pan in a counterclockwise spiral, starting from the outside edge of the pan.
10. Cover the pan and let the *ingera* cook until the edges begin to brown and curl up and the middle is dry, about 2 minutes.
11. Invert the pan over a clean dishtowel. The *ingera* should fall out of the pan. The first *ingera* may not turn out as well as the following ones.
12. Repeat the steps from number 8, until all the batter is gone.
13. They may be used immediately or, after they cool, they may be stored wrapped in plastic in the refrigerator for a few days.

cooking method good to use for Hopi wafer bread

◼ CLARIFIED SPICED BUTTER
(Ghee)

Unsalted butter consists of oil, solids, and water. Clarifying butter evaporates the water and separates the oil from the solids. The butter oil will keep indefinitely, unrefrigerated, without turning rancid. *Ghee* may be substituted for oil in any *zigni* to add richness and flavor.

1 pound unsalted butter
1-inch piece fresh ginger, peeled
¼ teaspoon dry basil
1 clove garlic
¼ teaspoon fenugreek
⅛ teaspoon cumin
¼ teaspoon turmeric
3 whole cloves
⅛ teaspoon celery seed
⅛ teaspoon coriander

YIELD: 1½ CUPS

1. Melt the butter in a pot over a low heat. Add all the other ingredients and cook uncovered over an extremely low heat for 45 minutes. Check the pot occasionally, but do not stir.
2. Skim off and discard any froth or spices floating on the surface. Remove the garlic and ginger pieces and discard them.
3. Allow the butter to cool to room temperature for 30 minutes. The white butter-solids and the spices will fall to the bottom of the pot and collect as sediment.
4. Dip the clear, golden butter out of the pot with a ladle, leaving all of the sediment behind.
5. Pour the clarified butter through a clean piece of cotton cloth stretched over the mouth of a jar to remove any remaining spice particles.
6. Store the clarified butter in a jar in a cool place.

🔳 SPICED LEGUME POWDER

(Shiro)

Shiro takes a long time to make. To speed things up, cook the legumes in four separate pots simultaneously, noting the different cooking times. This powder is used to make Legume Purée (see page 95.)

1 cup dried chickpeas
1 cup dried navy beans
2 cups dried yellow split peas
1 cup dried lentils
6 tablespoons *berbere* (Red Pepper Spice Mixture, page 19)
1½ tablespoons garlic powder
1 tablespoon salt

YIELD: 5½ CUPS POWDER

1. Soak the chickpeas in 2½ cups of cold water overnight, and drain. In another container, soak the navy beans in 3 cups of cold water overnight, and drain.
2. Put the chickpeas in a pot with 4 cups of water and cover the pot. Boil the chickpeas for about 1½ hours. Remove the pot from heat and drain any excess water. Set the chickpeas aside.
3. Put the beans in another pot with 4 cups of water. Partially cover the pot and boil for 1 hour. Drain any excess water and set the beans aside.
4. Place the split peas in a large pot with 8 cups of water. Partially cover the pot and boil 20 minutes. Drain the excess water and set the split peas aside.
5. Put the lentils in a pot and add 4 cups of water. Cover the pot partially and boil the lentils without stirring for 40 minutes. Drain the excess water and set the lentils aside.
6. Preheat the oven to 250°F. Spread each kind of legume on a baking sheet in a single layer. Roast the legumes in the oven for 2 hours, until they are all dry.

7. Grind the legumes together in a blender or a food processor until you have a fine powder. Add the *berbere*, garlic powder, and salt and grind until it is well blended.
8. Stored in an airtight container, this powder will keep for several months.

▓ EASY SPICED LEGUME POWDER

This recipe approximates the taste of authentic *shiro* powder without the lengthy preparation time. The flours may be found in natural food stores.

3 cups chickpea flour
1½ cups bean flour
1½ cups pea flour
5 tablespoons *berbere* (Red Pepper Spice Mixture, page 19)
2 tablespoons garlic powder
1 tablespoon salt

YIELD: 6 CUPS POWDER

1. Mix the chickpea, bean, and pea flours together. Add the *berbere*, garlic powder, and salt. Mix thoroughly.
2. Stored in an airtight container, the powder will keep for several months

Beverages

One of the most wonderful things to do in Eritrean towns is to visit the local cafés. In Asmara especially, many pleasant hours can be whiled away drifting from café to café, juice bar to juice bar. Eritrean juices, coffee, and tea are all served with a great deal of sugar. In the following recipes I use the quantity of sugar that will produce the most authentic Eritrean taste. However, you can decrease the amount to suit your own taste.

🔳 ERITREAN ORANGE JUICE
(Aranchi)

5 oranges
4 tablespoons sugar

YIELD: 32 OUNCES

1. Peel the oranges and separate them into sections.
2. Put them in a blender and add 2 cups of water, and the sugar.
3. Blend until frothy.
4. Strain and serve.

▨ ERITREAN PAPAYA JUICE

4 papayas
4 tablespoons sugar
1 lime, cut into wedges

YIELD: 32 OUNCES

1. Cut the papaya into quarters and scoop out the seeds. Cut off the skin and cut the papaya into pieces.
2. Put the papaya, 2 cups of water, and the sugar into the blender and blend.
3. Serve with a wedge of lime to squeeze into the juice. The juice will be rather thick.

▨ ERITREAN GUAVA JUICE
(Zeitün)

Guavas exist in several varieties. The Eritrean guava has pink flesh with white seeds dispersed in it. Called a strawberry guava in America, its botanical name is *Psidium cattleyanum*.

4 guavas
4 tablespoons of sugar

YIELD: 32 OUNCES

1. Cut the guavas in quarters and peel them. Cut the guavas in chunks and put them in a blender.
2. Add 2 cups of water and the sugar. Blend.
3. Strain the purée through a coarse sieve to extract the seeds, and discard them.
4. Pour into glasses and serve. The juice will be quite thick.

🈳 MIXED FRUIT JUICE
(Spriss)

I was sitting in a café one day, when a Dutch tourist approached me and showed me her glass. Looking puzzled, she asked, "Is this coffee?" Clearly, it was not. "Why, no," I said, "that's fruit juice." She told me that every day she asked for espresso, and she always received this. The juice was good, but she really would like some coffee. I told her the Tigrinya word for coffee was *bün*. It was only later that I realized when she asked for espresso, the waiter must have heard *spriss*, the Eritrean word for mixed fruit juice.

1 guava
2 bananas
1 papaya
1 orange
4 tablespoons sugar

YIELD: 32 OUNCES

1. Cut the guava in quarters, peel it, and put in a blender with 2 cups of water and blend.
2. Pour the guava purée through a coarse sieve to extract the seeds. Put the guava purée back into the blender.
3. Peel the banana, break it into pieces, and add it to the blender.
4. Peel and cut the papaya into quarters and scoop out the seeds. Cut the papaya into pieces, add them to the blender and blend.
5. Peel the orange, separate it into sections and add it to the other fruits.
6. Add the sugar and blend thoroughly. Strain the juice through a coarse sieve and serve. The juice will be quite thick.

▒ ESPRESSO

(Bün)

For this recipe you will need either a stove-top espresso pot or a modern electric espresso maker. For an electric espresso maker, follow the manufacturer's directions. The directions given below are for a stove-top espresso pot that holds 2½ cups of water.

6 level tablespoons dark-roasted Ethiopian
   finely ground coffee
4 tablespoons sugar

YIELD: 6 DEMITASSE CUPS
(18 OUNCES)

1. Separate the top and bottom of the pot and remove the basket.
2. Put 2½ cups of water into the bottom half. It will come to just below the safety valve.
3. Return basket to the bottom half, and fill it with the ground coffee, packing it down with the back of a spoon. The basket will be filled nearly to the top.
4. Screw the top half of the lid on tightly.
5. Place the pot over medium heat and allow it to boil until it stops sputtering and the top half of the pot is nearly full of coffee. This takes 5 to 10 minutes.
6. Put 2 teaspoons of sugar into each demitasse cup and fill it with espresso.

🏮 ESPRESSO WITH MILK
(*Macchiato*)

This is coffee "spotted" with milk, (the word for spotted in Italian is *macchiato*.) This drink is popular with elderly men who believe they are too frail for the undiluted espresso of their youth.

18 ounces espresso (page 30)
½ cup milk

YIELD: 6 DEMITASSE CUPS
(18 OUNCES)

1. Make 6 demitasse cups of espresso.
2. Heat the milk in a separate pot until bubbles form around the edge. Watch carefully or the milk will boil over and burn.
3. Use a spoon to drop a few spots of milk into the coffee, and serve.

" it is delicious "

▓ ESPRESSO WITH GINGER

In the north of Eritrea there lives a tribe called the Kunama. They drink coffee prepared with fresh ginger. It is delicious and it is said that once you become accustomed to it, you no longer like plain coffee. The directions given below are for a stove-top espresso pot that holds 2½ cups of water.

6 level tablespoons dark-roasted Ethiopian finely ground coffee
1 tablespoon peeled and minced fresh ginger
4 tablespoons sugar

YIELD: 6 DEMITASSE CUPS
(18 OUNCES)

1. Separate the top and bottom of the pot and remove the basket. Put 2½ cups of water into the bottom half. It will come to just below the safety valve.
2. Return basket to the bottom half, and fill it with the ground coffee and ginger. Pack it down with the back of a spoon. The basket will be filled nearly to the top.
3. Screw the top half of the lid on tightly.
4. Put the pot over medium heat and allow it to boil until it stops sputtering and the top half of the pot is nearly full of coffee. This takes 5 to 10 minutes.
5. Put 2 teaspoons of sugar into each demitasse cup and fill it with the coffee.

🈳 CAPPUCCINO

If you have a cappuccino machine, follow the manufacturer's instructions using dark-roasted Ethiopian finely ground coffee. Otherwise, follow the directions below.

18 ounces espresso (page 30)
3 cups milk, (whole or 2% work best;
    skim milk won't froth much)
4 tablespoons sugar

YIELD: 6 CUPS

1. Make espresso, but do not pour it into cups yet.
2. Heat the milk until little bubbles form around the edge of the pot. Watch carefully so it doesn't boil over and burn.
3. Pour the hot milk into a blender and blend briefly on high; this will froth the milk.
4. Fill each coffee cup with about ⅓ cup of espresso. Add 2 teaspoons of sugar and stir. Fill the rest of the cup with foamy milk and serve.

▨ ERITREAN TEA
(Shahi)

Eritrean tea is always brewed with sweet-smelling spices. There are two varieties of cardamom. One kind has a light green pod and the other has a white pod. The green is more aromatic and is the kind used in Eritrea.

12 cardamom pods
3 whole cloves
4 teaspoons black tea
4 tablespoons sugar

YIELD: 4 CUPS

1. Break open the cardamom pods and collect the seeds inside. Discard the pods.
2. Grind the cardamom seeds and cloves together, using a mortar and pestle or a coffee grinder, until you have a fine powder.
3. Boil 4 cups of water and add the loose tea and the cardamom mixture.
4. Remove the pot from the heat and steep the tea for 8 minutes.
5. Strain the tea into 4 cups and add 1 tablespoon of sugar to each cup.

takes 13 days

ERITREAN BEER
(Suwa)

Gesho is a kind of buckthorn shrub, with bitter leaves that have a taste similar to hops. Its botanical name is *Rhamnus phinoides*. One ounce (about 1 cup) of hops cones, available in beer-making stores, can be substituted for the gesho leaves. Making *suwa*, and allowing it to ferment takes thirteen days.

½ pound gesho leaves
1 pound wheat berries (whole-wheat kernels)
8 cups barley flour

YIELD: 6 QUARTS

1. Grind the gesho leaves in a blender or a food processor and put them into 8 cups of water and boil for about 15 minutes. Pour the boiled mixture into a large earthenware or glass container and add 16 cups (1 gallon) of water. Cover the container and let it stand for 6 days at room temperature, while you prepare the wheat berries.
2. Put the wheat berries in a covered container and add enough water to cover them. In about 3 days they will start to germinate. At that time, take them out of the water and place them in an empty container, cover it, and let them continue germinating at room temperature for 3 more days.
3. Remove the germinating wheat, spread it out on a baking sheet, and dry it in a 150°F oven for 1 hour, until they are crisp. Grind in a food processor, and add to the soaking leaves and water.
4. Mix the barley flour with 3 cups of water to make a dough. Spread it out on a baking sheet and bake it for about 10 minutes, until it browns on top.
5. Let it cool. Then break it into pieces and add it to the gesho leaves and wheat berry mixture in the container.
6. Let the container stand for an additional 7 days at room temperature.

7. At the end of that time, you will have a slightly alcoholic beverage. Before it can be served, it must be strained several times through a clean cloth.
8. Keep the *suwa* in the refrigerator, or bottle it. It will keep for several weeks.

▓ HONEY WINE *taken 11 days*
(*M'es*)

You may use 1 tablespoon of hops cones, (available at beer-making stores), in place of the gesho leaves. In Eritrea, this rather sweet wine is drunk from traditional long-necked glass containers that look a great deal like bud vases. *M'es* takes eleven days to prepare.

4 cups (32 ounces) honey
1 cup of gesho leaves

YIELD: 5 QUARTS

1. Mix the honey with 16 cups (1 gallon) of water and put it in a large glass container (such as a 2-gallon jar) and let it stand for 2 days at room temperature.
2. On the third day, place the leaves in a pot with 8 cups of the honey and water mixture. Bring it to a boil and simmer it for 20 minutes over a low heat.
3. Pour this boiled mixture back into the container of mixed honey and water and let it stand for an additional 7 days at room temperature.
4. Strain the mixture, discard the leaves. Cover the mixture and let it stand for another 2 days.
5. You may now strain the honey wine through a clean cloth and serve either at room temperature or chilled.

Breads

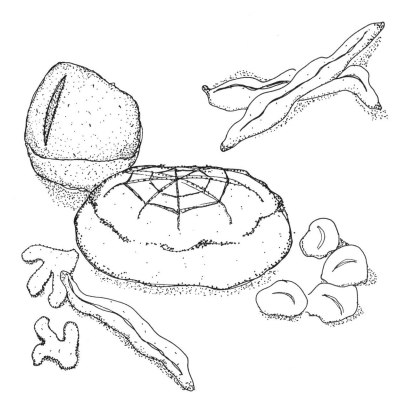

🔳 EVERYDAY ROLLS
(Panini)

This is the most basic of all bread doughs. It is made only from the four essential ingredients. These rolls can be eaten every day of the year in Eritrea, even during the fasting days required by the Eritrean Orthodox Church.

> 1 packet active dry yeast
> 3 cups warm water (about 110°F)
> 1 tablespoon sugar
> 1 teaspoon salt
> 7 cups flour

YIELD: 16 ROLLS

1. Dissolve the yeast in the water in a large mixing bowl. Add the sugar and salt. Stir.
2. Stir in the flour, 1 cup at a time. When the dough becomes too stiff to stir, work the flour in with your hands.
3. Knead the dough on a floured surface until it is elastic and no longer very sticky. This will take about 10 minutes.
4. Place the dough in a lightly oiled bowl and cover it with plastic wrap. Place the bowl in a warm place and allow the dough to rise for 1 hour.
5. Give the dough a sharp smack and knead it very briefly to get rid of any large air bubbles.
6. Divide the dough into 16 equal pieces, and form them into balls.
7. Grease 2 baking pans and arrange the rolls on the pans so that they do not touch each other. Cover them loosely with plastic wrap.
8. Put the baking pans in a warm place and allow the rolls to rise for 30 minutes. Preheat the oven to 350°F.
9. Remove the plastic wrap and place the pans in the oven and bake for 30 minutes.
10. Remove the rolls and place them on racks to cool.

▓ MILK ROLLS
(Pane al latte)

These slightly sweet rolls are usually eaten at breakfast or with coffee. They are fancifully shaped like three-fingered hands.

1 packet active dry yeast
3 tablespoons sugar
2 cups warm milk (about 105°F)
5¾ cups flour
1 egg
6 tablespoons butter, melted
1½ teaspoons salt

YIELD: 5 ROLLS

1. Dissolve the yeast and sugar in ½ cup of the milk in a large mixing bowl. Allow it to stand for 15 minutes. The mixture will become slightly foamy.
2. Stir in ¾ cup of the flour. Cover the bowl and leave it in a warm place for 1 hour.
3. Beat together the egg and remaining 1½ cups of milk in a separate bowl. Add this mixture to the large bowl.
4. Add the melted butter and salt and stir. Stir in the remaining 5 cups of flour, 1 cup at a time.
5. Turn the dough out onto a floured surface and knead it until it is soft and elastic. This will take about 10 minutes.
6. Place the dough in a lightly oiled bowl and cover it with plastic wrap. Place the bowl in a warm place and let it rise for 1 hour.
7. Give the dough a sharp smack and turn it out onto a floured surface. Knead it briefly to get rid of any large air bubbles. Grease 1 baking sheet.

8. Divide the dough into 5 equal pieces. Take one of the pieces and divide it into 4 equal pieces.
9. Form 1 of the 4 pieces into a ball. Form the other 3 pieces into short cylinders, about 3 inches long.
10. Attach the 3 cylinders to the ball, using a little water and pinching them. The rolls will look like small three-fingered hands.
11. Repeat this procedure with the remaining 4 pieces of dough. Arrange the 5 rolls on the greased baking pan, and cover loosely with plastic wrap.
12. Place the rolls in a warm place to rise for 45 minutes.
13. Preheat the oven to 350°F. Remove the plastic wrap and bake the rolls for 25 minutes.
14. Remove the rolls and cool them on racks.

▧ DENSE DINNER ROLLS
(Pane d'olio)

These compact rolls come in many strange shapes, although only one is described in this recipe. These rolls are only served with strongly-flavored meat dishes.

1 packet active dry yeast
½ cup warm water (about 110°F)
¼ cup olive oil
2 teaspoons salt
7 cups flour

YIELD: 6 ROLLS

1. Dissolve the yeast in the warm water in a large mixing bowl. Add 1½ cups of cool water, the olive oil, and salt. Stir.
2. Add 2 cups of the flour and stir. Continue adding flour 1 cup at a time. You will soon find it necessary to use your hands to work the flour in. Mix in all the flour. The dough will be extremely stiff and hard.
3. Let the dough rest for 5 minutes so the gluten will relax enough to allow the dough to be kneaded. Knead the dough on a floured surface until a smooth texture is achieved. This will take about 8 minutes.
4. Roll the dough out with a rolling pin. Fold the dough into quarters and roll out again. Continue folding and rolling for about 10 minutes.
5. Fold the dough up and allow it to rise in a covered bowl for 30 minutes. It will not rise very much.
6. Divide the dough into 6 equal pieces. Roll each piece out into a ribbon about 4 inches wide.

7. Roll the ribbon halfway up like a scroll. Then roll the other half of the ribbon up. Take one half of the scroll you have just made and rotate it 180 degrees. Thus, one half of the scroll will be facing up, and the other half will be facing down.

8. Repeat this procedure for the other 5 pieces of dough. Grease a baking pan. Arrange the rolls so that they don't touch.

9. Cover the rolls with plastic wrap, and put them in a warm place to rise for 1 hour. They will rise slightly.

10. Preheat the oven to 425°F. Bake the rolls for 5 minutes.

11. Brush the rolls with warm water and return them to the oven for another 5 minutes. Brush the rolls with warm water a second time and then bake for another 10 minutes.

12. Remove the rolls and cool on racks.

⚅ HARD ROLLS
(Banni)

These rolls are served with many dishes, where they are used instead of utensils to scoop up the food. They are best on the day they are baked.

3 cups warm water (about 110°F)
1 packet active dry yeast
2 teaspoons salt
2½ cups bran
5 cups flour

YIELD: 12 ROLLS

1. Pour the warm water into a large bowl. Add the yeast and salt. Stir.
2. Stir in the bran. Add the flour 1 cup at a time and work it in. You may find in the last stages of mixing that it is easiest to put aside the spoon and use your hands.
3. Knead the dough until it is springy and elastic. This takes about 5 minutes. If the dough feels sticky, knead in additional flour about a quarter of a cup at a time.
4. Place the dough in the bowl. Cover the bowl with plastic wrap and put it in a warm place to rise until the dough has approximately doubled in size, about 40 minutes.
5. Uncover the bowl and smack the dough smartly; it will deflate. Knead the dough briefly to rid it of any large air bubbles that may have formed.
6. Divide the dough in half. Divide each half into 3 equal pieces.
7. Flatten each piece into an oval about 8 inches long. Cut in half. This will make 12 roughly triangular pieces about 4 inches long.
8. Grease 2 baking pans and place 6 rolls on each baking pan. Cover them loosely with plastic wrap.
9. Put pans in a warm place to rise for 30 minutes. After 20 minutes, preheat the oven to 350°F.

10. Slash each roll before baking. With a serrated-edge knife make a cut across the dough about an inch from the previously-cut end and parallel to it. Cut about halfway through the dough.
11. Bake at 350°F for 30 minutes.
12. Remove the pans from the oven and cool the rolls on wire racks.

🔳 BREAD STICKS
(Grissini)

These are often served as an accompaniment to Italian meals.

1 packet active dry yeast
1½ cups warm water (about 110°F)
2 teaspoons salt *omit*
3 tablespoons oil *olive*
4 cups flour — *me ½ bread flr*

YIELD: 16 BREADSTICKS

1. Dissolve the yeast in the water in a large bowl.
2. Add the salt and oil and stir. Add the flour 1 cup at a time and work it in.
3. Knead the dough for 10 minutes on a floured surface until it is springy and elastic.
4. Place the dough in an oiled bowl, cover it, and put it in a warm place to rise until it has doubled in size, about 45 minutes.
5. Turn the dough out onto a floured surface and knead it briefly.
6. Grease 2 baking sheets. Roll out the dough on a floured surface into a rectangle about 16 inches by 6 inches.
7. Preheat the oven to 400°F.
8. Cut the rectangle of dough into 16 strips, each 6 inches long. Roll and elongate each strip, with your hands, until it is about 8 inches long.
9. Arrange 8 bread sticks on each cookie sheet about 1½ inches apart. They will expand slightly during baking.

10. Bake them for 15 minutes until they are golden brown and crisp.
11. Remove the bread sticks from the oven and cool them on a rack.

" delightful exotic flavi

❖ FESTIVE CARDAMOM BREAD

(H'mbasha)

This slightly sweet bread is made on special occasions and is
served with tea or coffee. It has a delightful, exotic flavor.

1 packet active dry yeast
3½ cups warm water (about 110°F)
¼ cup oil
3 tablespoons sugar
2 teaspoons salt
7½ cups flour
¼ cup raisins
½ teaspoon cardamom seeds (from about 16 pods,
    see page 34)

YIELD: 1 LARGE LOAF

1. Dissolve the yeast in the warm water in a large mixing bowl. Stir
   in the oil, sugar, and salt.
2. Add 2 cups of the flour and stir. Sprinkle the batter with the
   raisins and mix them in.
3. Sprinkle the batter with the cardamom seeds and mix them in.
4. Add the remaining 5½ cups of flour, 1 cup at a time, and mix it
   in. In the later stages you may find it easier to use your hands to
   incorporate the flour.
5. Turn the dough out onto a floured surface and knead it until it is
   springy and elastic. This will take about 10 minutes.
6. Put the dough in a covered bowl and place it in a warm place to
   rise for about 1 hour.
7. Give the dough a sharp smack and knead it briefly to remove any
   large air bubbles. Return it to the covered bowl and let it rise for
   1 hour more.

8. Preheat the oven to 400°F. Grease a pizza pan.

9. Give the dough a sharp smack and form it into a large, flat circle on the pizza pan.

10. Decorate the dough in a traditional way by slashing it with a serrated-edged knife. Slash lines about ¼ inch deep, radiating from a central point to the outside edge of the dough. Let rise for 30 minutes.

11. Place the pan in the oven and bake for 30 minutes.

12. Remove the bread from the oven and cool it on a rack.

Pastries

These pastries are available at any café in Asmara, and I spent a delightful few weeks trying them all. The pastries were always displayed in a glass case along one wall. A man stood behind the counter with tongs, waiting for my selection. Each of the pastries had the same price, the equivalent of seven cents. They were all different sizes, with myriad colors and shapes. Here are a few of my favorites.

🔹 SWEET BUNS   *"delicious"*

These buns are delicious plain, or you can split them open and fill them with whipped cream.

    1 packet active dry yeast
    1½ cups warm water (about 110°F)
    1 cup warm milk (about 105°F)
    ½ cup sugar
    1 egg, slightly beaten
    2 tablespoons oil
    2 teaspoons salt
    1 teaspoon vanilla
    5 cups flour
    4 tablespoons unsalted butter, melted

YIELD: 16 BUNS

1. Dissolve the yeast in the warm water in a large bowl. Add the warm milk and stir.
2. Add the sugar, egg, oil, salt, and vanilla and stir.
3. Add the flour 1 cup at a time, mixing after each cup. In the last stages of mixing it is easier to set aside the spoon and use your hands to mix.
4. Knead the dough with the heels of your hands until it is springy and elastic, about 10 minutes.

5. Place the dough in the bowl and set in a warm place to rise for about 1 hour.

6. Give the dough a sharp smack and turn it out onto a floured surface. Knead briefly.

7. Preheat oven to 350°F. Grease 2 cookie sheets.

8. Divide the dough into quarters, and divide each quarter into 4 equal pieces.

9. Form each piece into a ball and place 8 balls on each cookie sheet. Flatten them slightly, and put the cookie sheets in the oven.

10. After 20 minutes brush each bun with melted butter, using a pastry brush.

11. Bake the buns 5 minutes longer, then remove them from the oven and cool.

🔳 ITALIAN BUTTER COOKIES

These traditional cookies are served with coffee or tea.

1 cup unsalted butter, at room temperature
1 cup sugar
½ teaspoon salt
3 egg yolks ✓ *use whites* for ?
1 teaspoon vanilla extract
2½ cups flour
¾ cup raspberry or apricot jam

YIELD: 3 DOZEN COOKIES

1. Cream the butter and sugar together. Stir in the salt.
2. Add the egg yolks one at a time, mixing after each one. Add the vanilla and stir.
3. Stir in the flour, ½ cup at a time.
4. Preheat oven to 350°F. Grease 2 cookie sheets.
5. Form the cookie dough into balls that are about 1½ inches in diameter, and place them on the cookie sheets.
6. Flatten the balls slightly, and bake them for 10 minutes.
7. Remove the cookie sheets from the oven. Immediately make a shallow depression in the center of each cookie with the back of a spoon.
8. Place cookies on a rack to cool. When they are cool, place a spoonful of jam in the center of each cookie.

❧ HARD COOKIES
(Biscotti)

These slightly sweet cookies are an elegant accompaniment to any kind of coffee. They can be stored in an airtight container for up to 2 weeks.

2¾ cups slivered almonds
4 cups flour
2 teaspoons baking powder
¼ teaspoon baking soda
1 teaspoon cinnamon
⅔ cup sugar
1 cup orange juice
½ teaspoon lemon extract
¼ teaspoon almond extract
¾ cup oil
5 egg whites

YIELD: 40 COOKIES

1. Preheat oven to 350°F.
2. Combine the almonds, flour, baking powder, baking soda, cinnamon, and sugar in one bowl, and mix.
3. Combine the orange juice, lemon extract, almond extract, and oil in another bowl, and mix.
4. In a third bowl, beat the egg whites until they form stiff peaks.
5. Add the orange juice mixture to the dry ingredients and mix well. Fold in the beaten egg whites.
6. Grease 2 cookie sheets. Divide the dough in half. Form each half into a log about 3 inches wide and 15 inches long and place on the cookie sheets.
7. Bake for 40 minutes, then shut off the oven and remove the cookie sheets.
8. While the logs are still hot, carefully remove them from the cookie sheets to a cutting board; using 2 spatulas works well.

9. Cut each log into ¾-inch slices. Each log makes about 20 slices.
10. Put the slices back on the cookie sheets, making sure that none of them touch.
11. Put the cookies back into the oven. Turn the oven on to 200°F and bake them for 30 minutes.
12. Remove and cool the cookies before serving.

🈁 ERITREAN DOUGHNUTS

Although all the cafés in Asmara sold doughnuts, the best by far were sold at the Impero Café on Liberation Avenue. They were light and rich and warm, and like all the doughnuts in Eritrea, they were entirely unadorned, innocent of any sugar or glaze.

1 packet active dry yeast
½ cup warm milk (about 110°F)
½ teaspoon salt
1 cup cake flour
1 egg
¼ cup unsalted butter, melted
½ cup sugar
¼ teaspoon cinnamon
¼ teaspoon mace
1 cup all-purpose flour
6 cups oil

YIELD: 12 DOUGHNUTS

1. Dissolve the yeast in the milk in a large bowl. Mix in the salt and the cake flour. Put the bowl in a warm place for 40 minutes.
2. Mix in the egg and the melted butter. Combine the sugar, cinnamon, and mace in a separate bowl and stir it into the egg mixture.

3. Work in the all-purpose flour until you have a soft dough. Knead the dough for 5 minutes. Place the dough in a warm place to rise for 30 minutes.

4. Turn the dough out onto a floured surface and knead it briefly. Roll the dough out with a rolling pin until it is about ½ inch thick. If the dough is too sticky, you may add a little more flour.

5. Cut the dough with a doughnut-cutter or with 2 different-sized biscuit cutters. Place the cut-out doughnuts on an oiled surface. Repeat until all the dough has been rolled and cut out.

6. Cover loosely with plastic wrap and let the doughnuts rise for 1 hour. Heat the oil to about 365°F in a large pot. Put the doughnuts into the hot oil; using a pancake turner for this works well. Never have more than 3 doughnuts at a time in the oil.

7. After about 2 minutes, when the bottom of the doughnut is brown, turn it over and let it cook for another 2 minutes. Repeat until all the doughnuts have been cooked.

8. Drain the doughnuts on paper towels and serve.

🎏 TOMATO AND HERB PEPPER SQUARES
(Pizzette)

SAUCE:
> 2 tablespoons oil
> 3 cloves garlic, finely chopped
> 1 cup canned crushed tomatoes
> 1 teaspoon salt

DOUGH:
> 1 packet active dry yeast
> 1½ cups warm water (about 110°F)
> 1 teaspoon salt
> 3½ cups flour

TOPPING:
> 3 tablespoons olive oil
> 1 tablespoon red-pepper flakes
> 1 teaspoon dried oregano
> 1 teaspoon dried basil

YIELD: 12 PIECES

1. *To make the sauce:* Heat the oil in a saucepan. Sauté the garlic until the pieces begin to turn light brown. Add the crushed tomatoes and salt.
2. Simmer for 5 minutes, then remove the pot from heat and set it aside.
3. *To make the dough:* Dissolve the yeast in the warm water in a large bowl. Sprinkle in the salt and stir.
4. Add the flour one cup at a time, mixing after each cup.
5. Knead the dough with the heel of your hand until it is springy and elastic, about 10 minutes.
6. Put dough in a warm place to rise for about 30 minutes. Give the dough a sharp smack and turn it out onto a floured surface and knead briefly.

7. Roll out the dough with a lightly floured rolling pin until it is about the size of a baking sheet.

8. On a baking sheet with raised edges, pour 2 tablespoons of the olive oil and spread it evenly on the bottom and edges.

9. Lay the dough on the cookie sheet and stretch it with your fingers until it reaches the edges.

10. Preheat the oven to 450°F. Bake the dough for 10 minutes, and remove from the oven, leaving the oven on.

11. Brush the surface of the dough with remaining 1 tablespoon of olive oil, and spread a very thin layer of sauce on top.

12. Gently pierce the surface all over with a fork. Sprinkle the red-pepper flakes, oregano, and basil evenly over the surface of the dough.

13. Return it to the oven and bake it for another 10 minutes.

14. Remove from the oven and cut into 12 pieces. Serve.

Breakfasts

❄ BUTTERY SPICED CRUMBLED BREAD
(Fit'fit)

This is a scrumptious dish, eaten with the hands.

1½ cups butter
3 teaspoons of *berbere*
  (Red Pepper Spice Mixture, page 19)
6 cups of torn *ingera* pieces,
  (Flat Sourdough Bread, page 20) or other
  bread, with the crusts removed

YIELD: 4 SERVINGS

1. Melt the butter over a low heat, watching carefully so it does not burn. Add the berbere and stir constantly over a low heat for 1 minute.
2. Remove from the heat. Let stand for 5 minutes.
3. Return to the heat and warm the butter, stirring constantly, for 1 minute.
4. Pour the melted butter over the torn *ingera* in a large bowl. Mix vigorously, using a fork, until you have a quantity of buttery crumbs.
5. Eat, without utensils, by forming the crumbs into small balls with your fingers.

❧ YOGURT

Because the temperatures indicated must be precise, a thermometer is really a necessity for preparing this recipe. Make sure active cultures are indicated on the container of unflavored yogurt. Homemade yogurt must set for eight hours before it is ready to eat.

4 cups (1 quart) whole milk
1 tablespoon unflavored yogurt with
    active cultures

YIELD: 1 QUART YOGURT

1. Heat the milk to 180°F. Pour it into a glass or plastic container that has a lid.
2. Allow the milk to cool until it is 110°F. This will take between 15 and 25 minutes, depending on the temperature of the surrounding air.
3. Add the yogurt to the container and stir briefly. The yogurt will act as a starter, and will convert the milk to yogurt.
4. Cover the container and put it in a Styrofoam or insulated plastic picnic cooler. This will allow the milk to cool very slowly.
5. Leave the container undisturbed for 8 hours. After 8 hours the yogurt should have a custard-like consistency and a mildly sour flavor.
6. You may use it immediately, or refrigerate it and use it for up to a week. The yogurt will become somewhat more sour as it ages.

CRACKED WHEAT PORRIDGE

This porridge is often enjoyed for breakfast or as a snack.

1½ cups cracked wheat
1 cup milk
1 teaspoon salt
½ cup *ghee,* (Clarified Spiced Butter, page 22)

YIELD: 4 SERVINGS

1. Soak the cracked wheat in 3 cups of water for 1 hour, then drain.
2. Bring 1 cup of water, the milk and salt to a boil. Add ¼ cup of the *ghee.*
3. Slowly add the cracked wheat and cook over a low heat for 20 minutes, until the cracked wheat is soft.
4. Add the remaining ¼ cup of the *ghee* and serve hot.

✷ HARD ROLLS WITH RICOTTA AND HONEY

moyelas in Guatemala

This is a very pleasant breakfast which I often enjoyed with the early-morning sunshine streaming through the windows of one of my favorite cafés.

4 Hard Rolls (page 44)
1 cup ricotta cheese
½ cup honey

YIELD: 2 SERVINGS

1. Place 2 hard rolls, ½ cup of ricotta cheese and ¼ cup of honey on each plate.
2. Tear off a bite-sized piece of a roll, spread it with some ricotta cheese and top with a little honey.
3. Continue eating in this manner, resisting the urge to turn these ingredients into an efficient American sandwich.

🍽 MUSHROOM OMELET
(*Frittata di funghi*)

I use the common white button mushroom in this recipe, but any variety may be substituted.

6 eggs
½ teaspoon salt
¼ teaspoons black pepper
½ cup grated Parmesan cheese
½ cup finely chopped fresh parsley
3 tablespoons butter
8 white button mushrooms, cut in thin slices

YIELD: 3 SERVINGS

1. Beat the six eggs in a bowl and add the salt and pepper. Beat in the Parmesan cheese and parsley. Set aside.
2. Melt the butter in a large pan, and then remove from the heat. Arrange the mushroom pieces in a single layer in the pan, leaving a little space between them.
3. Sauté the mushrooms over a low heat, without stirring, for 5 minutes.
4. Pour the egg mixture over the layer of mushrooms and cook over a low heat until the eggs are set and the bottom of the omelet has turned golden. This will take about 5 minutes.
5. Turn the omelet over and allow the other side to cook for about 2 minutes.
6. Slice into 6 wedge-shaped pieces and serve 2 wedges to each person.

☒ SCRAMBLED EGGS WITH PEPPERS AND TOMATOES
(Frittata)

In Eritrea this is eaten without utensils. Instead, pieces of hard rolls are used to scoop up a bite.

8 eggs
1 large tomato, finely diced and drained
2 mild green peppers, seeded and finely diced
½ teaspoon salt
1 tablespoon oil

YIELD: 4 SERVINGS

1. Beat the eggs together and add the tomato, peppers, and salt.
2. Heat the oil in a pan over a low heat. Pour the egg mixture into the pan and cook for about 1 minute without stirring.
3. Stir the mixture gently and continue to stir for about 4 minutes until the eggs are cooked through but not dry.
4. Serve with Hard Rolls (page 44).

Snacks,
Appetizers,
and
Side Dishes

ROASTED CHICKPEAS

This tasty snack is sold in Eritrea much the same way that shelled peanuts are sold. Children carry quantities of them in baskets and sell a handful for a few cents. A girl scoops out some into your hand and then always, with traditional generosity, adds a few more. The chickpea sellers are always girls, while the peanut sellers are always boys.

½ pound dry chickpeas
1 teaspoon salt

YIELD: 2 CUPS

1. Put the chickpeas in a large pot with 4 cups of water. Bring the water to a boil, then remove the pot from the heat and allow the chickpeas to soak for 1 hour.
2. Drain the water from the chickpeas. Add another 4 cups of water to the pot and bring to a boil. Partially cover the pot and cook for 1 hour.
3. Drain the water and sprinkle the chickpeas with the salt. Stir thoroughly.
4. Preheat the oven to 250°F. Place the chickpeas in a single layer on a baking pan, and bake for 30 minutes.
5. Remove the baking sheet from the oven. Put the chickpeas in a bowl and cool. Serve as a snack.

⚅ ROASTED PUMPKIN SEEDS

When preparing any dish with pumpkin or other squash, keep the seeds and prepare this way for a crunchy snack.

1 pumpkin
1½ teaspoons salt

YIELD: 1½ CUPS

1. Cut the pumpkin in half and scoop out all the seeds. Place the seeds and fibers in a bowl with ½ cup of water.
2. Separate the seeds from the fibers with your hands and place the cleaned seeds in another bowl with ½ cup of water.
3. Spread the wet seeds in a single layer on a baking sheet. Sprinkle them generously with the salt.
4. Set the oven to 250°F. Place the baking sheet in the oven and roast the seeds for 45 minutes. Then shut the oven off and leave the baking pan in the oven until the oven is cool.
5. Remove the seeds and store them in an airtight container. The seeds may be eaten whole, or the outer shell may be removed and only the kernel eaten.

🔳 ERITREAN-STYLE POPCORN
(Im'baba eh'fün)

In Eritrea, popcorn is only eaten with coffee. The kernels are always eaten one at a time. Popcorn is a part of festive occasions and is sometimes thrown like confetti.

3 tablespoons oil
½ cup popcorn kernels
2 teaspoons salt
½ cup raisins

YIELD: 4 QUARTS

1. Heat the oil in a heavy pot over a medium-high heat. Add the popcorn kernels, cover, and shake the pot slightly to coat the kernels with oil.
2. Allow the kernels to heat for a few minutes until you hear them begin to pop. You may now lower the heat slightly.
3. Let the kernels pop, shaking the pot occasionally. When the kernels have stopped popping, remove the pot from heat.
4. Place the salt in a blender and grind it into a fine powder. This will approximate the finely ground salt powder that is commonly used in Eritrea.
5. Sprinkle the salt evenly onto the popcorn and mix it in thoroughly.
6. Pour the popcorn into a serving bowl. Add the raisins and stir them in.

⬛ SPICED BARLEY SQUARES

1 teaspoon ground cardamom
1 teaspoon ground ginger
1 teaspoon ground cloves
1½ teaspoons ground red pepper
1 teaspoon salt
1 cup unsalted butter, melted
3 cups barley flour

YIELD: 32 SQUARES

1. Combine the cardamom, ginger, cloves, red pepper, and salt. Mix well.
2. Stir the spice mixture into the melted butter in a bowl.
3. Add the barley flour and mix until you have a thick paste. Spread the paste out on a baking sheet, forming a rectangle about as big as the baking sheet.
4. Chill the paste in the refrigerator for 1 hour. Bake for 10 minutes at 350°F.
5. Cut the rectangle into 32 small squares with a pizza cutter or a knife. Serve as a snack.

✿ SPICY DIPPING SAUCE

(Sirsie)

This is one of my favorite foods. It is very easy, very spicy, and very satisfying.

¼ cup oil
1 onion, finely diced
4 cloves garlic, finely diced
4 teaspoons *berbere* (Red Pepper Spice Mixture,
    page 19)
6 tablespoons tomato paste
8 tablespoons plain yogurt, (optional)

YIELD: 4 SERVINGS

1. Heat the oil in a pot. Add the onion and sauté until it is soft and golden; this will take about 6 minutes.
2. Add the garlic and sauté for 1 minute more. Add the *berbere* and stir.
3. Add the tomato paste and 2½ cups of water. Cook over a low heat for about 5 minutes.
4. Serve in bowls with about 2 tablespoons of yogurt on top if desired. Eat by dipping in pieces of Hard Rolls (page 44) or other rolls and scooping up the sauce.

▓ CABBAGE SALAD WITH PEPPER DRESSING

This simple and tasty salad was served at my favorite pizza restaurant in Asmara. It was always given to me while I waited impatiently for my pizza.

½ cup vinegar
½ cup oil
½ teaspoon salt
¼ teaspoon ground black pepper
1 jalapeño pepper, seeded and minced
½ red sweet pepper, seeded and minced
1 cabbage, shredded

YIELD: 4 SERVINGS

1. Whisk together the vinegar, oil, salt, and pepper.
2. Stir in the minced peppers.
3. Pour the dressing over the cabbage in individual bowls and serve.

🏵 BLACK-EYED PEAS

This is a tasty and satisfying appetizer or snack that may also be
served as part of a cold buffet.

2½ cups (1 pound) dried black-eyed peas
3 tablespoons olive oil
½ teaspoon salt
2 onions, minced

YIELD: 6 SERVINGS

1. Place the black-eyed peas in a large pot with 8 cups of water.
   Bring the water to a boil, then cover the pot and remove from the
   heat. Let it stand for 1 hour.
2. Drain the water. Add another 8 cups of water to the black-eyed
   peas. Boil gently for 1 hour, and drain the remaining water.
3. Put the black-eyed peas in a bowl and pour the olive oil over
   them. Mix to coat them evenly with the oil. Sprinkle on the salt
   and mix thoroughly.
4. Reserve 2 tablespoons of the onion for garnish, and mix the rest
   into the peas. Let the mixture stand for 2 hours, so the flavors
   will blend.
5. Serve garnished with the reserved onion.

Have noticed that black-eyed kept in the fridge ff cooky lose flavo. Store in cupbd

▓ STUFFED MUSHROOM CAPS
(Capelle di funghi ripiene)

These make a delightful appetizer. Choose the largest mushrooms available.

12 white button mushrooms
½ teaspoon salt
½ teaspoon ground black pepper
3 tablespoons butter
¼ cup finely diced onion
½ cup finely chopped fresh parsley
1 clove garlic, finely diced
12 leaves fresh oregano, torn
4 leaves fresh sage, finely chopped
1 teaspoon paprika
⅛ teaspoon nutmeg
1½ cups dried bread crumbs
¼ cup vegetable broth
3 teaspoons olive oil

YIELD: 4 SERVINGS

1. Preheat the oven to 350°F. Remove the stem of each mushroom without breaking the cap. Chop the stems into pieces and sprinkle them with salt and pepper.
2. Sauté the pieces in the butter until they are soft. Add the onion and sauté until the onion is transparent.
3. Add the parsley, garlic, oregano, sage, paprika, and nutmeg, and cook for 5 minutes.
4. Add the bread crumbs and stir well. Stir in the broth.
5. Stuff each mushroom cap with the mixture. Grease a baking pan and arrange the stuffed caps in it. Lightly drizzle the olive oil over the stuffing of each cap.
6. Bake for 30 minutes. Serve warm.

🔳 FRIED MOZZARELLA

This was served as a main dish in the Italian restaurants of Eritrea. I recommend serving it as an appetizer.

1½ pounds mozzarella cheese, cut into
    20 rectangular sticks
¼ cup flour
1 egg
1 cup bread crumbs
3 cups oil

YIELD: 20 STICKS

1. Coat the mozzarella sticks with flour by shaking a few at a time in a clean paper bag filled with the flour.
2. Beat together the egg and 2 tablespoons of water in a shallow bowl. Dip the floured mozzarella sticks in the egg mixture.
3. Roll the sticks in the bread crumbs to coat them. Chill the breaded sticks for 30 minutes in the refrigerator.
4. Heat the oil in a large pan to 375°F. Lower a few sticks into the oil with a slotted spoon. Remove them from the oil after about 2 minutes, when the crumbs are golden.
5. Repeat the process until all the sticks have been fried. Drain them on paper towels and serve warm.

▦ SHRIMP IN SPICED BUTTER

This is a delectable and unusual way to prepare shrimp.

1 cup of *ghee* (Clarified Spiced Butter, page 22)
1 teaspoon of *berbere* (Red Pepper Spice Mixture,
      page 19)
1 pound of raw shrimp, peeled and deveined

YIELD: 4 SERVINGS

1. Preheat the oven to 300°F. Warm the *ghee* in a saucepan and mix in the *berbere*.
2. Put the shrimp in a baking dish. Pour the butter mixture over them.
3. Put the pan, uncovered, into the oven and let the shrimp bake for about 15 minutes, spooning the butter mixture over the shrimp every 5 minutes.
4. When the shrimp are pink and opaque, remove them from the oven and serve.

🔳 ROASTED POTATOES

This simple dish is commonly served with sautéed greens as an accompaniment to a meat or fish dish.

¼ cup oil
4 large potatoes, peeled and quartered
1 teaspoon salt
½ teaspoon ground black pepper

YIELD: 4 SERVINGS

1. Preheat the oven to 350°F.
2. Pour the oil into a baking dish and add the potatoes. Turn the potatoes in the oil until they are well coated.
3. Sprinkle the potatoes evenly with the salt and pepper.
4. Bake for 1 hour until the potatoes are golden brown, crispy on the outside and soft in the middle.

▨ SAUTÉED SWISS CHARD
(Costa)

This dish is traditionally made with fresh Swiss chard. However, frozen may be substituted. Use only 20 ounces; defrost and drain the leaves thoroughly, but don't cut them up.

3 bunches (about 40 ounces) Swiss chard, washed
3 tablespoons oil
6 cloves garlic, sliced
½ teaspoon salt

YIELD: 4 SERVINGS

1. Cut the long stalks of the leaves into 1-inch pieces. Cut or tear the leaves into pieces.
2. Place the leaves and stalks in a steamer in a large pot over ½ inch of boiling water. Steam for 8 minutes, then remove from heat and set aside.
3. Heat the oil in a large pan. Sauté the garlic until it begins to turn golden.
4. Add the leaves and stalks. Stir well to coat with the oil and garlic.
5. Sauté for 5 minutes. Sprinkle the Swiss chard with salt and serve.

SAUTÉED MUSTARD GREENS

(Homli)

Either fresh or frozen mustard greens may be used. For frozen, use only 20 ounces. Defrost and drain the leaves thoroughly, then follow the instructions from number 2 on.

3 bunches (about 40 ounces) fresh mustard greens, washed
3 tablespoons oil
6 cloves garlic, sliced
½ teaspoon salt

YIELD: 4 SERVINGS

1. Cut or tear the leaves into pieces. Put them in a steamer in a large pot over ½ inch of boiling water. Cover the pot and steam the greens for 5 minutes. Remove from the heat and set them aside.
2. Heat the oil in a large pan. Sauté the garlic until it starts to turn golden. Add the mustard greens, and use a fork to separate the damp leaves slightly.
3. Stir the greens well to coat them with the oil and garlic.
4. Sauté the greens for about 5 minutes, stirring occasionally.
5. Sprinkle them with salt and serve.

🈁 SAUTÉED SPINACH GREENS
(Spinaci)

This is best made with fresh spinach. If you use frozen spinach, 30 ounces is enough. Defrost and drain the leaves thoroughly, then follow the instructions from number 2 on.

3 bunches (about 40 ounces) fresh spinach, washed
3 tablespoons oil
6 cloves garlic, sliced
½ teaspoon salt

YIELD: 4 SERVINGS

1. Cut off and discard the stems of the spinach leaves. Set the leaves aside.
2. Heat the oil in a large frying pan and sauté the garlic slices until they begin to turn golden. Add the spinach leaves to the pan.
3. Stir the leaves well to coat with the oil and garlic. Cover the pan and cook over a medium heat for 1 minute.
4. Uncover the pan and cook the leaves for 5 minutes more, stirring occasionally, until they are soft and dark green.
5. Sprinkle the spinach with salt and serve.

🔲 FRIED MUSHROOMS
(Funghi fritti)

In Eritrea mushrooms are enormous, wild, and only available for two weeks after the rainy season in August. The caps are often 9 or 10 inches across. However, these are not frequently seen in America, so this recipe uses the common, white button mushroom.

12 fresh white button mushrooms
2 eggs
1½ cups of dried bread crumbs
1 cup oil

YIELD: 4 SERVINGS

1. Slice each mushroom lengthwise, through the middle of the stem and the cap. Cut a slice off of each cap, so that you have 2 additional crescent-shaped pieces.
2. Beat the eggs with 1 tablespoon of water in a shallow bowl. Dip each piece of mushroom into the beaten egg mixture, and then coat it with the bread crumbs.
3. Lay the pieces in a single layer on wax paper and refrigerate them for 15 minutes.
4. Heat the oil in a large pan and fry the pieces of mushroom in a single layer. You may need to cook more than one batch. When the breading turns golden, remove them and drain on paper towels. Serve warm.

Traditional Eritrean Main Dishes

🔳 LENTILS IN SAVORY SAUCE

(Tum'tumo)

In Eritrea, this is a popular dish during the fasting periods required by the Eritrean Orthodox Church. It can be eaten during those times because it does not use any meat or dairy products.

2 cups dried lentils
1 onion, finely chopped
¼ cup oil
1 teaspoon salt
¼ teaspoon *berbere* (Red Pepper Spice Mixture, page 19)
1 tomato, chopped
1 tablespoon tomato paste
2 cloves garlic, minced

YIELD: 4 SERVINGS

1. Put the lentils in a large pot with 6 cups of water. Bring the water to a boil, then reduce the heat. Cover the pot partially and allow it to simmer for about 15 minutes, until the lentils are soft. Set the lentils aside.
2. Sauté the onion in the oil in a large pot until the onion is soft and golden.
3. Add the salt, *berbere*, tomato, tomato paste, and ½ cup of water. Mix well and cook for 1 minute.
4. Add the garlic and lentils. Stir and bring to a boil.
5. Serve in bowls and eat with bread or *ingera* (Flat Sourdough Bread, page 20).

✿ MILD PUMPKIN STEW
(D'ba alicha)

When pumpkin is not available, any winter squash may be substituted. The stew is flavorful, but milder than the Spicy Pumpkin Stew, (page 89).

¾ cup oil
2 onions
3 cloves garlic, minced
2 teaspoons peeled, minced fresh ginger
½ teaspoon turmeric
6 cups peeled, diced pumpkin (use an 8-inch pumpkin)
2 sweet green peppers, seeded and diced

YIELD: 6 SERVINGS

1. Heat the oil in a pot. Add the onions and sauté until golden.
2. Add the garlic, ginger, turmeric, and 7 cups of water. Bring to a boil.
3. Add the pumpkin and cook 15 minutes.
4. Add the green peppers and cook for 5 minutes. Serve.

⚅ SPICY PUMPKIN STEW
(D'ba zigni)

Three acorn squashes may be substituted for the pumpkin.

⅓ cup oil
1 onion, finely diced
4 teaspoons *berbere* (Red Pepper Spice Mixture, page 19)
6 cups peeled, diced pumpkin (use an 8-inch pumpkin)
3 tablespoons tomato paste
2 teaspoons salt

YIELD: 4 SERVINGS

1. Heat the oil in a pot. Add the onion and sauté until golden.
2. Remove the pot from the heat. Add the *berbere* and stir.
3. Add the pumpkin to the pot, and mix well to coat each piece with the spices.
4. Return the pot to the stove, and add 2 cups of water. Simmer for 15 minutes.
5. Add 2 cups of water and the tomato paste, and salt. Stir. Simmer for 15 more minutes until the pumpkin is cooked.
6. Serve with *ingera* (Flat Sourdough Bread, page 20) or bread.

❧ MILD ACORN-SQUASH STEW
(Hum'hum alicha)

This recipe uses no meat or dairy products.

½ cup oil
1 onion, finely chopped
2 cloves garlic, minced
2 teaspoons peeled, minced fresh ginger
2 acorn squash, peeled and diced
2 carrots, chopped
½ teaspoon salt
½ teaspoons ground cloves
½ teaspoon cinnamon

YIELD: 4 SERVINGS

1. Heat the oil in a pot. Add the onion and sauté until golden.
2. Add the garlic, ginger, and 5 cups of water. Bring to a boil and add the squash. Cook for 10 minutes.
3. Add the carrots, salt, cloves, and cinnamon. Cook over medium heat for another 10 minutes. Serve.

🔳 MIXED VEGETABLES IN CURRY SAUCE

(Alicha)

This is a wonderful vegetarian stew.

1 cauliflower, separated into florets
2½ teaspoons salt
1½ cups (½ pound) fresh or frozen string beans
1 onion, finely diced
½ cup oil
2 stalks celery, chopped
3 carrots, cut in circles
2 potatoes, diced
1 tablespoon curry powder
1 chili pepper, seeded and minced
½ cup finely chopped fresh parsley
3 cloves garlic, minced

YIELD: 6 SERVINGS

1. Boil the cauliflower in 7 cups of water with 1 teaspoon of the salt for about 15 minutes. Drain the water and set the cauliflower aside.
2. Boil the string beans in 3 cups of water with ½ teaspoon of the salt for about 10 minutes. Drain the water and set the string beans aside.
3. Sauté the onion in the oil in a large pot until the onion is soft and golden.
4. Add the celery, carrots, and potatoes and cook for 5 minutes while stirring.
5. Add the cooked cauliflower and string beans. Stir well.
6. Add the curry powder, chili pepper, parsley, and garlic. Mix thoroughly.
7. Add the remaining 1 teaspoon of salt and 6 cups of water.
8. Cook for about 25 minutes until the potatoes and carrots are cooked.
9. Serve with bread or *ingera* (Flat Sourdough Bread, page 20).

❦ BREAD SOUP
(Ingera mirek)

Although *ingera* is traditionally used, in this recipe, eight slices of bread with the crusts removed may be substituted.

2 tablespoons oil
1 onion, diced
½ teaspoon curry powder
1 stalk celery, diced
2 tomatoes, diced
1 soup bone
½ teaspoon salt
4 *ingera* rounds (Flat Sourdough Bread, page 20)

YIELD: 4 SERVINGS

1. Heat the oil in a pot. Add the onion and sauté until golden.
2. Add the curry powder and stir. Add the celery, tomatoes, soup bone, salt and 3 cups of water.
3. Bring the soup to a boil, then reduce the heat and allow it to simmer for 40 minutes.
4. Remove the soup bone. Purée the mixture in a blender.
5. Tear the *ingera* into small pieces and place an equal amount of torn *ingera* in each bowl.
6. Pour the soup over the *ingera* and stir briskly with a fork to break the *ingera* into fragments. Serve.

"Extremely delicious"

✤ BEAN STEW
(*Fül*)

keeps + reheats

This extremely delicious dish is very common throughout Eritrea, in the tiny villages as well as the larger towns. You can get it at any little restaurant. It is easy to make, and keeps and reheats beautifully.

In Eritrea, this is eaten without utensils. If you want to be truly authentic, serve each bowl of *fül* with two Hard Rolls (page 44); tear off pieces and scoop up the stew. It's a little untidy, but a lot of fun.

3 tablespoons oil
1 large onion, finely diced
¾ teaspoon *berbere* (Red Pepper Spice Mixture, page 19)
2 cups dried fava or pinto beans, soaked overnight
   and drained
1 teaspoon salt
⅛ teaspoon black pepper
¼ teaspoon dried oregano
1 tomato, diced
2 Anaheim chili peppers, seeded and diced

fava

YIELD: 4 LARGE SERVINGS

1. In a large pot, heat the oil and sauté the onion until it is golden. Stir in the *berbere*.
2. Add the beans and 4 cups of water; bring to a rolling boil. Then decrease the heat until it simmers.
3. Cover the pot and simmer for at least 1 hour, or until beans are tender. Check occasionally to see that the beans are still covered with water. If they are not, add more water.
4. Remove 2 cups of cooked beans and put them in a blender. Add 1 cup of hot water and purée.
5. Pour the purée back into the pot and bring the mixture to a boil for 5 minutes.
6. Remove the pot from heat. Add the salt, pepper, and oregano. Stir.
7. Serve in bowls, garnished with pieces of tomato and peppers.

▓ BEAN STEW WITH SARDINES
(Asa fül)

The only place this dish is available is in Massawa, a city on the Red Sea where fish is a staple. In Eritrea, this is served with two Hard Rolls (page 44) which are torn into pieces and used to scoop up the stew. Spoons are not used.

3 tablespoons oil
1 large onion, finely diced
¾ teaspoon *berbere* (Red Pepper Spice Mixture, page 19)
2 cups dried fava or pinto beans, soaked overnight,
    and drained
2 cans (4⅜ ounces each) sardines in oil,
    drained and chopped
1 teaspoon salt
⅛ teaspoon black pepper
¼ teaspoon dried oregano
1 tomato, diced
2 Anaheim chili peppers, seeded and diced

YIELD: 4 LARGE SERVINGS

1. In a large pot, heat the oil and sauté the onion until it is light brown. Stir in the *berbere*.
2. Add beans and 4 cups of water; bring to a rolling boil. Then decrease the heat until it is simmering.
3. Cover the pot and simmer for at least 1 hour, or until the beans are tender. Check occasionally to see that the beans are still covered with water. If they are not, add more water.
4. Remove 2 cups of cooked beans and put them in a blender. Add 1 cup of hot water and purée.
5. Pour the purée back into the pot. Add the sardines and stir. Bring the mixture to a boil for 5 minutes.
6. Remove the pot from heat. Add salt, pepper, and oregano. Stir.
7. Serve in bowls, garnished with pieces of tomato and peppers.

🔳 LEGUME PURÉE
(Shiro)

In Eritrea this is usually served on a large communal platter. Several ladles of *shiro* are placed on a large round *ingera* (Flat Sourdough Bread, page 20) and several *ingera*, folded in quarters, are placed nearby. Each person tears off pieces of *ingera* and scoops up some *shiro*. Outside Eritrea, it may also be served with flour tortillas, or with bread.

    1 onion, finely diced
    3 tablespoons oil
    1⅓ cups Spiced Legume Powder (page 23 or page 24)

YIELD: 4 LARGE SERVINGS

1. Sauté the onion in the oil in a large pot until onion is golden.
2. Remove pot from heat and add 4 cups of water. Return to the heat and heat the mixture to simmering.
3. Add the spiced legume powder, and stir with a fork or whisk to eliminate any lumps.
4. Cook for about 5 minutes until it begins to bubble and thicken. Serve.

▦ SPICY BEEF STEW
(Tsega zigni)

For extra flavor and richness, replace the oil with *ghee* (Clarified Spiced Butter, page 22).

½ cup oil
1 onion, finely diced
3 teaspoons *berbere* (Red Pepper Spice Mixture, page 19)
1 pound beef stew meat, cut into ½-inch cubes
3 tablespoons tomato paste
1 teaspoon salt

YIELD: 4 SERVINGS

1. Heat the oil in a pot. Add the onion and sauté it until it is golden.
2. Add the *berbere* and stir. Add the beef to the pot, and mix well to coat each piece with the onion and spice mixture.
3. Cook over a low heat, stirring, for 3 minutes.
4. Add the tomato paste and 4 cups of water to the pot. Add the salt and mix well.
5. Bring the stew to a boil, then reduce the heat and simmer for 25 minutes.
6. Serve with *ingera* (Flat Sourdough Bread, page 20) or another bread.

🔳 ZESTY STEWED CHICKEN
(Doro zigni)

This is often served on holidays and festive occasions. It is traditional for Easter.

1 whole chicken
4 cups finely chopped onion
¾ cup *ghee* (Clarified Spiced Butter, page 22) or oil
5 teaspoons *berbere* (Red Pepper Spice Mixture, page 19)
2 heaping tablespoons tomato paste
1 teaspoon salt
6 hard-boiled eggs, peeled

YIELD: 6 SERVINGS

1. Cut the chicken into the traditional Eritrean 12 parts: 2 breasts, 2 thighs, 2 legs, the back, the neck, and the wings. Divide the wings below the humerus so you have 4 wing pieces. Set the chicken aside.
2. Sauté the onions in the *ghee* until they are soft and golden.
3. Add the *berbere* and stir. Stir in 1 cup of water.
4. Add the pieces of chicken and mix well to coat them with the spiced mixture.
5. Stir in another 1 cup of water and cook over a medium heat for 20 minutes.
6. Add the tomato paste, salt, and 4 cups of water and stir.
7. Place the hard-boiled eggs in the pot and simmer uncovered for 20 minutes. The sauce will thicken.
8. Serve with *ingera* (Flat Sourdough Bread, page 20) or another bread.

▦ LAMB STEW SEASONED WITH SPICES
(Be'geh zigni)

For greater flavor and richness, replace the oil with *ghee* (Clarified Spiced Butter, page 22).

½ cup oil
1 onion, finely diced
2 teaspoons *berbere* (Red Pepper Spice Mixture, page 19)
1 pound lamb stew meat, cut into ½-inch cubes
1 potato, diced
2 tablespoons tomato paste
½ teaspoon salt

YIELD: 4 SERVINGS

1. Heat the oil in a pot. Add the onion and sauté until golden.
2. Add the *berbere* and stir. Add the pieces of lamb to the pot, and mix well to coat each piece with the onion and spice mixture.
3. Cook over a low heat, stirring, for 5 minutes.
4. Add the potato and stir well. Add the tomato paste and 4 cups of water to the pot. Add the salt and mix well.
5. Bring the stew to a boil, then reduce the heat and allow it to simmer for 20 minutes.
6. Serve with *ingera* (Flat Sourdough Bread, page 20).

▨ PIQUANT FISH STEW
(Asa zigni)

For this recipe you may use cod, sole, flounder, or any other available fish.

½ cup oil
1 onion, finely diced
3 teaspoons *berbere* (Red Pepper Spice Mixture, page 19)
2 pounds fresh fish filets, cut into ½ inch pieces
3 tablespoons tomato paste
1 teaspoon salt

YIELD: 4 SERVINGS

1. Heat the oil in a large pot. Add the onion and sauté until soft and golden.
2. Add the *berbere* to the pot and stir briefly. Add the fish and cook for 5 minutes over a low heat, stirring gently.
3. Add the tomato paste, salt, and 4 cups of water. Cook, uncovered, for 15 minutes.
4. Serve with *ingera* (Flat Sourdough Bread, page 20) or another bread.

▓ ERITREAN CHOPPED MEAT ½ inch piece of meat
(Kulu'wa)

Although many Eritrean meat dishes are highly spiced, this one is a flavorful, but not very spicy, delicious preparation.

3 tablespoons unsalted butter
1 onion, finely diced
1 tomato, finely diced
2 cloves garlic, finely diced
½ teaspoon *berbere* (Red Pepper Spice Mixture, page 19)
1 pound top round beef, cut into ½-inch pieces
½ teaspoon salt
¼ teaspoon pepper

YIELD: 4 SERVINGS

1. Melt the butter in a large frying pan. Sauté the onion until it is golden.
2. Add the tomato, garlic, and *berbere*. Stir.
3. Add the meat and sauté, stirring often, for about 10 minutes. The liquid will evaporate and the meat will be flavored with the vegetable mixture.
4. Serve with bread or *ingera* (Flat Sourdough Bread, page 20).

🔳 SPICED CABBAGE STEW
(*Kablo zigni*)

⅓ cup oil
1 onion, finely diced
4 teaspoons *berbere* (Red Pepper Spice Mixture, page 19)
1 cabbage, finely chopped
3 tablespoons tomato paste
1 teaspoon salt

YIELD: 4 SERVINGS

1. Heat the oil in a pot. Add the onion and sauté until golden.
2. Remove the pot from heat. Add the *berbere* and stir.
3. Add the cabbage to the pot, and mix well to coat thoroughly.
4. Return the pot to the heat and add 2 cups of water. Bring to a boil and simmer for 15 minutes.
5. Add the remaining 2 cups of water and the tomato paste, and salt. Stir, and simmer for another 10 minutes, and serve with *ingera* (Flat Sourdough Bread, page 20) or other bread.

■ FIERY POTATO STEW
(D'nish zigni)

½ cup oil
1 onion, finely diced
4 teaspoons *berbere* (Red Pepper Spice Mixture, page 19)
6 medium potatoes, peeled and diced into ½-inch pieces
4 tablespoons tomato paste
1 teaspoon salt

YIELD: 4 SERVINGS

1. Heat the oil in a pot. Add the onion and sauté until golden.
2. Remove the pot from the heat. Add the *berbere* and stir.
3. Add the potatoes to the pot, and mix well to coat each piece of potato.
4. Return the pot to the stove, and add 2 cups of water. Simmer for 10 minutes.
5. Add 2 cups of water (or enough to just cover the potatoes) the tomato paste, and salt and stir. Simmer for 10 more minutes until the potatoes are cooked.
6. Serve with *ingera* (Flat Sourdough Bread, page 20) or another bread.

Italian-
Eritrean
Main Dishes

🔳 ERITREAN PIZZA

This is a delicious, slightly spicy pizza. The addition of *berbere* to the sauce gives it the true Eritrean taste.

PIZZA DOUGH

    1 packet dry active yeast
    1 cup of warm water (about 110°F)
    1 teaspoon salt
    3 tablespoons oil
    3 cups flour

SAUCE

    2 tablespoons oil
    2 cloves garlic, minced
    ¼ teaspoon *berbere* (Red Pepper Spice Mixture, page 19)
    2 tablespoons tomato paste
    ¼ teaspoon salt
    ¼ teaspoon dried oregano
    ¼ teaspoon dried basil
    1½ cups shredded mozzarella cheese
    1 tomato, chopped and drained
    1 green pepper, seeded and diced

YIELD: 1 16-INCH PIZZA

1. *To make the dough:* Dissolve the yeast in the warm water. Add the salt and oil. Stir. Work in the flour.
2. Turn the dough out onto a floured surface and knead until it is springy and elastic, about 10 minutes. You may add a little more flour if the dough is too sticky.
3. Put the dough in a bowl and cover it with plastic wrap. Place the bowl in a warm place and let it rise until it has doubled in size, about 45 minutes.
4. Give the dough a sharp smack and knead it briefly to destroy any large air bubbles.

5. Rub a 16-inch pizza pan with a little oil and stretch the dough out on it so it reaches the edges. Set it aside.

6. *To make the sauce:* Heat the oil in a pot and add the garlic. When the garlic begins to turn golden, add the *berbere* and stir. Add the tomato paste, salt, oregano, and basil. Stir.

7. Add 1 cup of water and mix thoroughly. Allow the sauce to simmer for 10 minutes, the remove from the heat.

8. Preheat the oven to 500°F. Spread the sauce on the prepared pizza dough. Sprinkle on the mozzarella cheese. Arrange the chopped tomato and green pepper on top.

9. Place the pizza pan in the oven and bake for 15 minutes. Remove the pizza, slice, and serve.

▓ FRESH TOMATO PIZZA

This is a simple Eritrean version of pizza that is delicious, though uncommon in America.

PIZZA DOUGH:
    1 packet active dry yeast
    1 cup warm water (about 110°F)
    1 teaspoon salt
    3 tablespoons oil
    3 cups flour

TOPPING:
    10 ripe plum tomatoes, chopped and drained
    20 fresh basil leaves, torn
    ½ pound mozzarella cheese, sliced

YIELD: 1 16-INCH PIZZA

1. Dissolve the yeast in the warm water. Add the salt and oil and stir. Work in the flour.
2. Turn the dough out onto a floured surface and knead until it is springy and elastic, about 10 minutes.
3. Put the dough in a bowl and cover it with plastic wrap. Place the bowl in a warm place and let it rise until it has doubled in size, about 45 minutes.
4. Give the dough a sharp smack and knead it briefly to get rid of any large air bubbles.
5. Stretch the dough out on a lightly oiled 16-inch pizza pan so it reaches the edges.
6. Preheat the oven to 500°F. Cover the dough with the tomatoes and arrange the basil leaves on top of them.
7. Cover the tomatoes and basil with the slices of mozzarella cheese. Bake the pizza for 15 minutes, until the cheese is melted and the crust is golden.
8. Remove the pizza from the oven, slice, and serve.

▓ SPAGHETTI WITH ZIGNI SAUCE

This is the quintessential blending of Eritrean and Italian cuisine. It can be made with meat, or see page 109 for a meatless *zigni* sauce.

½ pound ground beef
3 tablespoons oil
2 onions, finely diced
2 teaspoons *berbere* (Red Pepper Spice Mixture, page 19)
½ cup tomato paste
½ teaspoon salt
1 pound dried spaghetti

YIELD: 4 SERVINGS

1. Thoroughly brown the ground beef in a pan over low heat. This will take about 10 minutes. Drain off the fat and discard. Set the ground beef aside.
2. Heat the oil in a pot. Add the onion and sauté until golden.
3. Add the *berbere* and stir. Add the ground beef and stir for a few minutes while it cooks with the spices.
4. Stir in the tomato paste. Add 1½ cups of water and stir.
5. Cover the pot and let the sauce simmer for 20 minutes. Add the salt, stir, and simmer for 3 minutes more.
6. Prepare the spaghetti according to package instructions, and serve the sauce over it.

🔳 SPAGHETTI WITH MEATLESS ZIGNI SAUCE

¼ cup oil
2 onions, finely diced
3 cloves garlic, minced
2 teaspoons *berbere* (Red Pepper Spice Mixture, page 19)
½ teaspoon salt
1 tomato, finely diced
½ cup tomato paste
1 pound dried spaghetti

YIELD: 4 SERVINGS

1. Heat the oil in a pot. Add the onions and sauté until golden.
2. Add the garlic and stir. Add the *berbere* and salt and cook over a low heat for 1 minute while stirring.
3. Add the diced tomato and cook for another 5 minutes, stirring occasionally.
4. Add the tomato paste and 1½ cups of water and mix well. Simmer for 10 minutes.
5. Prepare the spaghetti according to package instructions and serve the sauce over it.

▓ SPAGHETTI WITH FRESH TOMATOES AND BASIL

This dish is known in Eritrea as spaghetti "invalid-style." Long-time Italian residents of Eritrea believe this is an appropriate meal when they are feeling ill, because this dish is not very rich. This may not be medicinally accurate, but it is a light and delicious way to prepare pasta.

> 1 pound dried spaghetti
> 8 tomatoes
> 20 fresh basil leaves, torn into small pieces
> 8 teaspoons olive oil
> 4 tablespoons grated Parmesan cheese

YIELD: 4 SERVINGS

1. Prepare the spaghetti according to package instructions. Arrange equal portions on 4 plates.
2. Chop the tomatoes into medium cubes, and reserve the juice. Divide equal portions of chopped tomatoes and juice among the four plates.
3. Arrange equal amounts of basil leaves on the tomatoes and drizzle 2 teaspoons of olive oil over each plate of spaghetti.
4. Sprinkle on equal portions of Parmesan cheese and serve.

🞈 SPAGHETTI WITH EGG AND ITALIAN BACON

(Spaghetti alla carbonara)

This recipe calls for Italian *pancetta*, which is the same cut of pork as bacon, and it is cured, but not smoked. You can find it in Italian specialty stores.

3 cloves garlic, sliced
3 tablespoons oil
½ pound *pancetta* (Italian bacon) sliced into slivers
½ cup dry white wine
2 teaspoons salt
1 pound dried spaghetti
3 eggs
1 cup grated Parmesan cheese
1 cup finely chopped fresh parsley
½ tablespoon freshly ground black pepper

YIELD: 4 SERVINGS

1. Sauté the garlic in the oil in a large pan. Watch carefully as the pieces of garlic begin to get lightly browned, then remove them from the oil and set them aside.
2. Fry the slivers of *pancetta* in the same oil until they begin to get crisp.
3. Add the white wine and the garlic pieces to the pan. Simmer for about 3 minutes, then remove the pan from the heat.
4. Boil water in a large pot, add the salt and prepare the spaghetti according to package instructions. Drain the spaghetti and return it to the pot.
5. Beat the eggs together with the Parmesan cheese and parsley in a separate bowl and add the mixture to the spaghetti.
6. Heat the spaghetti and egg mixture over a low heat while mixing thoroughly. It is important to heat the mixture to 165°F to avoid any possibility of salmonella.

7. Quickly heat the *pancetta* and wine mixture until it is very hot, add it to the spaghetti and mix thoroughly.

8. Sprinkle on the black pepper and serve.

✥ SPAGHETTI WITH MIXED SAUCES
(*Spaghetti al sugo misto*)

This pasta is served with two sauces in separate bowls, a thick meat sauce and a thinner, smooth tomato sauce. Each person takes as much of each sauce as he desires. It is a very satisfying meal.

MEAT SAUCE:

4 tablespoons oil
1 small potato, finely diced
2 onions, finely diced
1 stalk celery, finely diced
2 cloves garlic, sliced
1 anchovy fillet
1 pound ground beef
¼ cup tomato paste
½ cup red wine
2 cups (16 ounces) canned chopped tomatoes
2 bay leaves
1½ teaspoons salt
¼ cup chopped black olives

TOMATO SAUCE:

3 cloves garlic, sliced
4 tablespoons oil
1 onion, finely diced
2 tablespoons tomato paste
2 cups (16 ounces) canned chopped tomatoes
2 slices white bread with crusts removed
1 teaspoon salt
1 teaspoon paprika
1 teaspoon dried basil
½ teaspoon dried oregano
¼ teaspoon very finely chopped lemon peel

1½ pounds dried spaghetti
6 tablespoons grated Parmesan cheese
6 tablespoons grated Romano cheese

YIELD: 6 SERVINGS

1. *To make the meat sauce:* Heat the oil in a large pan and brown the potato. Add the onion, celery, and garlic. Stir.
2. Mash the anchovy fillet and stir it in. Cook the vegetable mixture over a medium heat for about 20 minutes, until the vegetables are soft.
3. Add the ground beef to the pan and cook, stirring occasionally, until the meat has changed from red to brown, and then until the meat is browned a little further. This will take about 10 minutes.
4. Add the tomato paste to the pan. Mix 1½ cups of water and the wine together in a separate container and then gradually add this mixture to the pan and stir.
5. Add the chopped tomatoes and bay leaves and partially cover the pan. Simmer for 20 minutes.
6. Remove the bay leaves and add the salt and black olives. Simmer briefly.
7. *To make the tomato sauce:* In a large pan, gently sauté the garlic in oil. Add the onion and sauté until it is golden.

8. Transfer the garlic and onion to a blender and blend them with 1 cup of water. Return the mixture to the pan.

9. Blend the tomato paste and chopped tomatoes in the blender and add them to the pan.

10. Blend the white bread and 1 cup of water in the blender and add the mixture to the pan.

11. Add the salt, paprika, basil, oregano, and lemon peel to the pan. Simmer for 20 minutes.

12. Prepare the spaghetti according to package directions. Mix the Parmesan and Romano cheeses together and put them in a bowl to be used as garnish. Serve.

🔳 BROILED RED SEA GROUPER

Grouper comes in many sizes, from just a few pounds to a giant fish weighing sixty pounds or more. The flesh is bland, white, and meaty. If grouper is not available, any very fresh ocean fish may be substituted.

1 (5-pound) grouper, cleaned, with the head and tail left on
6 cloves garlic, slivered
4 teaspoons paprika
2 navel oranges
2 teaspoons salt
1 lemon
8 teaspoons *berbere* (Red Pepper Spice Mixture,
    page 19)

YIELD: 4 SERVINGS

1. Wash the fish inside and out. Make 6 very small cuts on each side of the fish and insert slivers of garlic beneath the skin. Rub the skin with the paprika.
2. Wash 1 of the oranges and cut it into thin slices, leaving the peel on. Arrange the slices all along the cavity of the fish, allowing them to overlap. Sprinkle the orange slices with the salt and the remaining garlic slivers.
3. Broil the fish for about 15 minutes on each side.
4. Cut the remaining orange and the lemon into quarters. Serve the fish in filets, with a quarter of orange and lemon for each serving.
5. At each serving, place a small bowl containing 2 teaspoons of *berbere*. Each diner can dip up a little *berbere* with a piece of orange or lemon and rub it on the fish to make it as spicy as he likes.

✿ BREADED CUTLETS
(Capretto)

In Italian, *capretto* means goat and in Eritrea this very common dish is made with goat meat. However, as it is nearly impossible to find goat meat in America, this recipe uses lamb. The taste is similar.

4 thin slices center-cut lamb leg (about 2 pounds)
¼ teaspoon salt
¼ cup flour
1 egg, beaten
½ cup bread crumbs
½ cup oil

YIELD: 4 SERVINGS

1. Trim the fat from the slices. Remove the bone and cut the slices in half; sprinkle the slices with the salt.
2. Coat the slices with the flour. Mix the egg and 2 tablespoons of water together in a shallow bowl.
3. Dip the floured slices of lamb in the egg mixture. Coat the slices with the bread crumbs.
4. Put the coated slices in the refrigerator and chill them for 15 minutes. Preheat the oven to 200°F.
5. Heat ¼ cup of the oil in a large pan. Sauté 4 of the pieces for 2 minutes on one side and turn them over. Sauté the pieces for 2 minutes on the other side.
6. Turn the pieces back over and sauté them for 5 minutes more.
7. Remove the pieces to a baking dish and place in the oven to keep them warm while the remaining pieces are sautéed.
8. Heat the remaining ¼ cup of oil in the pan. Sauté the remaining slices in the same manner.
9. Arrange all the slices on a platter and serve.

🔡 ROAST PIGEON
(*Piccione arrostito*)

Because pigeons are not commonly eaten in America, Cornish hens may be substituted.

6 pigeons
6 slices *pancetta* (Italian bacon)
6 tablespoons butter
1½ teaspoons salt
1 teaspoon black pepper
1 teaspoon dried oregano
2 bunches parsley
1½ cups meat broth

YIELD: 6 SERVINGS

1. Preheat the oven to 350°F. Clean the birds and stuff each one with 1 slice of *pancetta*.
2. Rub the skin of each bird with 1 tablespoon of butter. Combine the salt, pepper, and oregano. Sprinkle each bird with this mixture.
3. Cut enough parsley to make 1 cup of finely chopped leaves. Use the remaining parsley stalks and leaves to line the bottom of a roasting pan.
4. Place the birds in the roasting pan. Sprinkle them with the chopped parsley.
5. Cover the pan and roast for 20 minutes. Then uncover the pan and roast for an additional 10 minutes, until the breasts are tender.
6. Baste the birds with the meat broth and roast for an additional 5 minutes.
7. Remove the birds from the roasting pan and serve.

❧ BREADED CHICKEN CUTLETS

Because you cannot buy this cut of chicken, you will have to get a whole chicken and create this cut yourself. You may use the rest of the chicken for the broth in my recipe for Long Thin Noodles in Broth (page 119).

1 whole chicken
¼ cup unsalted butter, melted
¼ teaspoon salt
¼ teaspoon pepper
½ cup bread crumbs
½ cup oil

YIELD: 2 SERVINGS

1. Remove each breast of the chicken leaving the humerus (the first joint of the wing) attached. Scrape off the meat from the lower end of the humerus so the piece of chicken resembles a cutlet.
2. Pound the breast with a wooden mallet to flatten it slightly. Dip each cutlet in melted butter and sprinkle it with salt and pepper.
3. Coat each one with bread crumbs. Chill them in the refrigerator for 20 minutes.
4. Preheat the oven 350°F. Heat the oil in a pan and sauté each cutlet for 2 minutes on each side, until the crumbs are golden.
5. Place them on a baking sheet and put them in the oven for 8 minutes to finish cooking. Remove and serve.

unforgettable ✓

🎴 LONG THIN NOODLES IN BROTH *a soup*
(*Capelli d'angelo in brodo*)

This is an unforgettable dish. I know a man who ate it thirty years ago in Asmara, and he is *still* talking about it. It is light and delicate and is served as a first course in a traditional Italian meal. It is a soup that never loses its appeal.

BROTH: *me: use beef*

1 whole chicken
2 whole cloves
1 medium onion
1 clove garlic, peeled
2 parsnips, peeled
1 small tomato
1 small bunch parsley
1 bay leaf
3 egg whites *egg whites*
½ teaspoon salt

NOODLES:

3 cups unbleached flour
½ cup grated Parmesan cheese *(in the dough)*
3 egg yolks
2 tablespoons olive oil

YIELD: 6 SERVINGS

1. *To make the broth:* Wash the chicken and put it in a large stockpot with 12 cups of cold water.
2. Push the cloves into the onion and add it to the pot. Add the garlic, parsnips, tomato, parsley, and bay leaf.
3. Bring the stock to a boil and simmer for 2 hours. Do not cover the pot. Occasionally skim off the foam that accumulates on top.
4. Remove the chicken and use it for some other dish. Remove the cloves, bay leaf, and the parsley and discard them.

5. Put the boiled onion, garlic, parsnips, and tomato into a food processor or blender and purée. Return the purée to the stockpot and refrigerate the broth overnight.

6. Remove the pot from the refrigerator. The soft, yellow chicken-fat will have risen to the top of the broth and solidified. Skim it off and discard it.

7. Strain the cold broth through a fine strainer.

8. Remove ½ cup of broth to a bowl and add 3 egg whites, and mix thoroughly.

9. Return the broth and egg white mixture to the stock-pot. Simmer the broth for about 10 minutes. The egg whites will coagulate and trap the remaining fine particles in the broth.

10. Stretch a moistened cloth over the top of a large bowl and pour the broth through the cloth. The broth should now be completely clear.

11. Add the salt and stir.

12. *To make the noodles:* Make a mound on a tabletop of the flour and grated cheese.

13. Make a well in the center of the mound and drop in the egg yolks, and oil.

14. Mix the ingredients with your hands until you have a smooth dough.

15. Knead the dough until it has a supple and elastic consistency, about 10 minutes.

16. If you have a pasta machine, roll the dough on the finest setting, and cut it into the finest strips. If you are working by hand, roll and stretch the dough until it is as thin as possible, then cut it into very fine strips.

17. *To cook the long thin noodles in broth:* Bring the broth to a boil and add the pasta.

18. Allow the pasta to cook for about 2 minutes.

19. Put equal portions of the noodles into 6 bowls. Ladle the soup over the noodles and serve.

3 layers of lasagne

Italian Eritrean Main Dishes 🔲 121

🔲 LASAGNA

This is a very substantial and satisfying repast. It is <u>so delicious</u> that it is worth the time and trouble it takes. This recipe yields many servings and is suitable for a gathering.

MEAT SAUCE:
- ¼ cup oil
- 1 onion, finely diced
- 1 teaspoon *berbere* (Red Pepper Spice Mixture, page 19) *omit*
- 4 fresh tomatoes, diced
- 3 cloves garlic, minced
- ½ cup finely cut parsley leaves *It. parsley*
- 1 cup tomato paste *no liquid?*
- 1 teaspoon dried oregano
- 1 teaspoon dried basil
- 2 teaspoons salt
- 1½ pounds ground beef *+ pepper see "me" note*

FILLING:
- 4 cups (2 pounds) ricotta cheese
- 1 cup finely cut fresh parsley leaves *It. parsley*
- 1 teaspoon salt
- 1 teaspoon ground black pepper
- ½ cup grated Parmesan cheese *Reggiano*
- ¾ cup <u>milk</u>
- 1 egg

- 20 lasagna noodles (about 1 pound)
- 1 tablespoon oil
- 3 cups (1 pound) shredded mozzarella cheese

YIELD: 10 SERVINGS

1. *To prepare the meat sauce:* Heat the oil in a large pot and sauté the onion until it begins to turn golden. Add the *berbere* and stir.

2. Add the diced tomatoes, garlic, and parsley. Cook over a low heat while stirring for 2 minutes. Add the tomato paste and 2½ cups of water and mix well.

3. Mix in the oregano, basil, and 1½ teaspoons of the salt. Cover the pot and allow it to simmer for 10 minutes while you prepare the ground beef.

4. Put 2 tablespoons of water in a dry frying pan. Add the ground beef and the remaining ½ teaspoon of salt and cook over a low heat while stirring until the meat loses its red color, about 4 minutes.

5. Drain the fat from the meat. Add the meat to the tomato sauce and mix it in well.

6. Cover the sauce and allow it to simmer for 30 minutes. Set it aside.

7. *To prepare the filling:* In a large bowl mix together the ricotta cheese, parsley, salt, pepper, and Parmesan cheese.

8. In a separate bowl, beat together the milk and egg and stir it into the ricotta cheese mixture. Continue to stir until the mixture is smooth and creamy. Set it aside.

9. Prepare the lasagna noodles according to package directions, adding 1 tablespoon oil to the water. Drain the noodles, separate them and dry them on clean towels.

10. Preheat the oven to 350°F. Spread ½ cup of the meat sauce over the bottom of a 9-inch × 13-inch baking dish. *9 X 13*

11. Cover the sauce with a single layer of noodles, overlapping them *no* slightly. Spread 2 cups of the meat sauce over the noodles. Cover the meat sauce with 1½ cups of the ricotta cheese mixture. Sprinkle 1 cup of mozzarella cheese over that.

12. Cover the mozzarella cheese with another layer of noodles placed perpendicular to the first layer of noodles. This will help to hold the lasagna together.

13. Repeat the layers of meat sauce, ricotta cheese mixture, and mozzarella cheese. Place a third layer of noodles over the mozzarella cheese, again perpendicular to the layer below.

14. Continue to put on the layers of meat sauce, ricotta cheese mixture, and mozzarella. Cover the mozzarella cheese with a final layer of noodles, again laid perpendicular to the layer below.

perpendicular = at rite angles

15. Top the noodles with the remaining meat sauce and mozzarella cheese. Cover the baking dish with aluminum foil and bake it for 40 minutes. @ 350 ?
16. Remove the foil and bake the lasagna for an additional 5 minutes.
17. Remove the lasagna from the oven and allow it to cool for 10 minutes. Cut and serve.

note: me:
when the pan has been filled,
cut into squares.
In between squares:
1 pepper the peppers [illegible]
crisp
2. Ground extra
3. Mix with [illegible]
[illegible] in cracker
Pour into some
later squares

me: Saute pepper-then peppers are
crisp. Dry on paper towel. Ground &
add to "meat Sauce" before cooking
sauce.

Desserts

🔆 FRUIT SALAD
(Macedonia di frutta)

This is the most common dessert offered in Eritrean restaurants. It never seems to vary, no matter where you eat. The grenadine syrup is manufactured locally by the Asmara Wine and Liquor Company.

    2 bananas, peeled and sliced
    1 guava, peeled and cubed
    1 papaya, peeled, seeded, and cubed
    2 oranges, peeled and cut in pieces
    ¾ cup grenadine

YIELD: 4 SERVINGS

1. Divide equal portions of each fruit into 4 bowls.
2. Drizzle 3 tablespoons of grenadine syrup over each portion.
3. Mix gently and serve.

🔳 CUSTARD WITH CARAMELIZED SUGAR
(Crème Caramel)

This sweet is a very popular dessert served in Eritrea's Italian restaurants. For some unknown reason it is always served with a giant spoon.

CARAMEL COATING:
¼ cup sugar

CUSTARD:
1 cup plus 3 tablespoons milk
⅓ cup sugar
2 eggs
⅛ teaspoon salt
¾ teaspoon vanilla

YIELD: 6 SERVINGS

1. *To make the caramel coating:* Heat ¼ cup sugar in a heavy pot over a low flame. Watch carefully and stir constantly as the sugar begins to melt.

2. Continue stirring and slowly heating until the liquid sugar is the color of maple syrup. Be sure not to let the sugar burn.

3. Remove the pot from the heat. Spoon 2 teaspoons of the liquid sugar into 1 individual custard cup, or you may use a 6-cup muffin tray.

4. Tilt the muffin tray so the liquid sugar coats the inside of the muffin cup. If you are using a muffin tray, it is easiest to coat the cups one at a time.

5. One at a time, repeat steps 3 and 4 for the remaining five muffin cups. Set the muffin tray aside. The caramel coating will harden.

6. *To make the custard:* Preheat the oven to 325°F.

7. Combine the milk, sugar, eggs, salt, and vanilla in a bowl and beat until the mixture is frothy.

8. Pour equal amounts of the mixture into each of the muffin cups.

9. Place a rack in a baking pan and place the muffin tray on the rack. Pour very hot, (not boiling,) water into the baking pan so the water rises about 1 inch around the cups.
10. Set the whole pan with rack, water, and muffin tray into the oven and bake for 50 minutes. Test for doneness by inserting a knife blade into the custard. If it comes out clean the custard is done.
11. Remove the muffin tray and chill it for at least 1 hour.
12. When the tray is entirely chilled, dip 1 muffin cup in very hot water for a moment or two. Invert muffin cup over a small plate. If the custard does not unmold easily, slide a knife blade between the custard and side of the muffin cup and push gently.
13. Repeat the unmolding process for the remaining 5 cups.
14. Refrigerate them until they are served.

▦ BANANAS FLAMBÉ

This dessert combines crackling caramelized sugar and soft, sweet bananas.

4 bananas, sliced
1 cup sugar
½ cup brandy, 80 proof or higher

YIELD: 4 SERVINGS

1. Coat the banana slices with ½ cup of sugar. Divide the banana slices into 4 equal portions in Pyrex or other heat-proof dishes. Set them aside.
2. Mix ½ cup of sugar with ¼ cup of water in a heavy pot. Heat the syrup over a low heat, stirring constantly. The syrup will begin to bubble.
3. Continue heating until the mixture has turned the color of maple syrup. Watch carefully so it does not burn.
4. Pour equal portions of the caramelized syrup over each portion of sliced bananas. This must be done quickly because the syrup hardens soon after being removed from the heat.
5. Warm the brandy briefly, to make it more volatile. Pour 2 tablespoons of brandy over each portion and light it with a flame.
6. Allow the brandy to burn away and serve.

🔡 FLAMED JAM OMELET

This is a dramatic dessert, served after a light meal.

6 eggs
4 tablespoons milk
2 teaspoons flour
4 tablespoons unsalted butter
8 teaspoons jam
1 tablespoon sugar
1 cup brandy (at least 80 proof)

YIELD: 4 OMELETS

1. Beat the eggs, milk, and flour together. Melt 1 tablespoon of butter in a small frying pan.
2. Pour ¾ cup of the egg mixture into the pan. Cook it over a moderate flame until the omelet is nicely set.
3. Spoon 2 teaspoons of jam along the middle of the omelet. Fold each side over the jam.
4. Slide the omelet onto a plate. Repeat the process for the other 3 omelets.
5. Place all 4 omelets in a pan large enough to hold them all easily. Sprinkle them with the sugar.
6. Put the pan on a low heat. Carefully pour the brandy into the pan and ignite it. The burning alcohol will make a big ball of blue flame, so exercise caution.
7. Leave the pan on the stove until the flames have gone out. Spoon the warm liquid over the omelets and serve.

no bake

▨ ITALIAN RUM CHEESECAKE

no bake

This cheesecake requires no baking. Overnight refrigeration transforms dry, crunchy ladyfingers and moist ricotta-raspberry filling into an amazingly delicious dessert.

> 4 cups (2 pounds) ricotta cheese
> ½ cup dark rum
> ¾ cup sugar
> 1 cup fresh or frozen raspberries
> 18 ladyfingers
> 1 cup heavy whipping cream
> 1 tablespoon whole raspberries for garnish
>
> YIELD: ONE 8 × 8-INCH CAKE

1. Beat together the ricotta cheese, rum, and ½ cup of the sugar in a large bowl.
2. Purée the raspberries with the remaining ¼ cup of sugar in a blender or food processor.
3. Add the raspberry purée to the ricotta cheese mixture and stir briefly.
4. Cover the bottom of an 8-inch square casserole dish with a layer of ladyfingers. You may break some of the ladyfingers in half in order to cover the bottom of the dish completely.
5. Pour about half of the ricotta cheese mixture over the ladyfingers, and spread it evenly.
6. Cover with another layer of ladyfingers, again breaking some of them in half if necessary.
7. Pour the rest of the mixture on top of the ladyfingers and spread it evenly, making sure all of the ladyfingers are well covered.
8. Cover the dish with plastic wrap and place it in the refrigerator for 24 hours.
9. Immediately before serving, whip the cream until it forms stiff peaks and spread it on top of the cake. Garnish with the whole raspberries and serve.

🔡 FROZEN ALMOND CONFECTION *Sartoni*
(Biscuit tortoni)

This is a very delicate, pretty confection, appropriate for a festive dessert.

1 cup half-and-half
1 teaspoon vanilla extract
¼ teaspoon almond extract
5 tablespoons superfine sugar
¼ teaspoon salt
1 cup crushed almond-flavored cookies
1½ cups heavy whipping cream
2 tablespoons slivered almonds

YIELD: 6 SERVINGS

1. Stir together the half-and half, vanilla extract, almond extract, sugar and salt in a large bowl. Mix in the crushed cookie crumbs.
2. Set the mixture aside for 1 hour, until the cookie crumbs have soaked up the half-and-half.
3. In a separate bowl, whip the cream into soft peaks. Fold the whipped cream into the cookie-crumb mixture.
4. Place a foil baking cup into each cup of a 6-cup muffin tray. Spoon equal portions of the whipped cream mixture into the cups. Place the muffin tray in the freezer. Freeze for 3 hours.
5. Toast the slivered almonds by placing them in a dry frying pan and stirring them constantly over a medium heat for 3 minutes, until they begin to turn light brown. Let them cool.
6. Remove the muffin tray from the freezer and garnish each cup with the toasted almonds.
7. Place each foil cup on a small plate and serve.

⊠ COFFEE ICES
(*Graniti di espresso*)

This is a sophisticated dessert that takes several hours to freeze. It has a unique crystalline texture.

¼ cup superfine sugar
¼ cup boiling water
1¾ cups espresso, chilled
1 cup heavy whipping cream
2 tablespoons crème de cacao

YIELD: 4 SERVINGS

1. Dissolve 3 tablespoons of the sugar in the boiling water. Stir this sugar syrup into the chilled espresso.
2. Pour the coffee mixture into a freezer tray, or a loaf pan and cover it with foil. Place it in the freezer and freeze for 6 hours.
3. Place 4 individual dessert cups in the freezer to chill.
4. Remove the coffee mixture and stir it with a fork to break up any large ice-crystals. Return it to the freezer and freeze it for another 1 hour.
5. Whip the cream until it forms soft peaks. Sprinkle on the remaining 1 tablespoon of sugar and continue to whip the cream for about 30 seconds, until it forms stiff peaks.
6. Remove the coffee slush from the freezer and stir in the crème de cacao. Add the slush to the whipped cream and beat them together.
7. Spoon equal amounts of the mixture into the chilled dessert cups. Return them to the freezer for another 2 hours.
8. Remove from the freezer and serve.

🔃 ERITREAN TRIFLE
(Zuppa Inglese)

Although this is called *zuppa Inglese*, which in Italian means
"English soup," it is really not a soup at all. Rather, it is a very beautiful dessert, pretty enough to be the centerpiece of a table. For best
appearance, it should be served in a clear glass or plastic bowl approximately 8 inches in diameter and 5 inches deep.

12 ladyfingers
½ cup rum or peach brandy
1 (3.9-ounce) package vanilla pudding mix
5⅔ cups half-and-half (about 3 pints)
½ teaspoon vanilla extract
2 cups fresh raspberries *or* 2 cups of sliced bananas
1 (3.9-ounce) package pistachio pudding mix
¼ cup crushed unsalted pistachios
⅓ cup grenadine
⅛ teaspoon salt
2 tablespoons cornstarch
2 cups whipping cream
¼ cup slivered almonds

YIELD: 8 LARGE PORTIONS

1. Moisten the ladyfingers with the rum. Arrange them against the
    inside of the bowl, leaving spaces between them.
2. Prepare the vanilla pudding according to package instructions,
    but substitute 2 cups of half-and-half in place of milk, and add
    ½ teaspoon vanilla extract.
3. Fill the bottom third of the bowl with the vanilla pudding.
4. Arrange 1 cup of the raspberries on top of the vanilla pudding.
5. Prepare the pistachio pudding according to package instructions,
    but substitute 2 cups of half-and-half in place of milk and stir in
    the pistachios.
6. Fill the middle third of the bowl with pistachio pudding, and
    arrange the remaining cup of raspberries on top of it.

7. Make pomegranate pudding by whisking together the grenadine, the remaining 1⅔ cups of half-and half, salt, and cornstarch. Heat it over a low heat while stirring constantly for 8 minutes, until it comes to a boil and thickens.

8. Fill the top third of the bowl with the pomegranate pudding to within an inch of the top. Place the bowl in the refrigerator to chill for 3 hours.

9. Whip the cream until it forms stiff peaks and pile it above the top of the bowl. Sprinkle the whipped cream with the almond slivers and serve.

Recipe Index

chich peas 69

African Cookbooks from Hippocrene . . .

BEST OF REGIONAL AFRICAN COOKING
Harva Hachten
Here is a gourmet's tour of Africa, from North African specialties like Chicken Tajin with Olives and Lemon to Zambian Groundnut Soup and Senegalese Couscous. Over 240 recipes that deliver the unique and dramatic flavors of each region: North, East, West, Central and South Africa.
274 pages • 5½ x 8½ • 0-7818-0598-8 • W • $11.95pb • (684)

TRADITIONAL SOUTH AFRICAN COOKERY
Hildegonda Duckitt
A collection of recipes culled from two previous books by the author, this volume provides ideas for tasty, British- and Dutch-inspired meals and insight into daily life of colonial Africa.
178 pages • 5 x 8½ • 0-7818-0490-6 • W • $10.95pb • (352)

TASTES OF NORTH AFRICA: Recipes from Morocco to the Mediterranean
Sarah Woodward
Over 100 recipes represent an exquisite mélange of cultures, histories and ingredients from Morocco to Spain, Portugal, Sicily and Provençe. With 23 full pages of stunning food and travel photography.
160 pages • 8½ x 9½ • 0-7818-0725-5 • $27.50hc • NA • (187)

International Cookbooks from Hippocrene . . .

WORLD'S BEST RECIPES
From Hippocrene's best-selling international cookbooks, comes this unique collection of culinary specialties from many lands. With over 150 recipes, this wonderful anthology includes both exotic delicacies and classic favorites from nearly 100 regions and countries.
256 pages • 5½ x 8½ • 0-7818-0599-6 • W • $9.95pb • (685)

ART OF SOUTH AMERICAN COOKERY
Myra Waldo
This cookbook offers delicious recipes for the various courses of a typical South American meal. Dishes show the expected influence of Spanish and Portuguese cuisines, but are enhanced by the use of locally available ingredients.
266 pages • 5 x 8½ • b/w line drawings • 0-7818-0485-X • W • $11.95pb • (423)

THE ART OF BRAZILIAN COOKERY

Dolores Botafogo

Includes over 300 savory and varied recipes, ranging from Churasco (barbe-cued steak) and Vatapa (Afro-Brazilian fish porridge from the Amazon) to sweets, and aromatic Brazilian coffees.

240 pages • 5½ x 8½ • 0-7818-0130-3 • W • $11.95pb • (250)

A SPANISH FAMILY COOKBOOK, REVISED EDITION

Juan and Susan Serrano

Over 250 recipes covering all aspects of the Spanish meal, from tapas (appe-tizers) through pasteles (cakes and pastries). Features a new wine section, including information on classic Spanish sherries and riojas.

244 pages • 5 x 8½ • 0-7818-0546-5 • W • $11.95pb • (642)

BEST OF GREEK CUISINE: COOKING WITH GEORGIA

Georgia Sarianides

Chef Georgia Sarianides offers a health-conscious approach to authentic Greek cookery with over 100 tempting recipes. Also includes helpful sections on Greek wines, using herbs and spices, and general food preparation tips.

176 pages • 5½ x 8½ • b/w line drawings • 0-7818-0545-7 • W
• $19.95hc • (634)

GOOD FOOD FROM AUSTRALIA

Graeme and Betsy Newman

A generous sampling of over 150 Australian culinary favorites. "Steak, Chops, and Snags," "Casseroles and Curries," and "Outback Cooking" are among the intriguing sections included. In time for the 2000 Olympics in Sydney!

284 pages • 5½ x 8½ • b/w line illustrations • 0-7818-0491-4 • W
• $24.95hc • (440)

THE JOY OF CHINESE COOKING

Doreen Yen Hung Feng

Includes over two hundred kitchen-tested recipes and a thorough index.

226 pages • 5½ x 7½ • illustrations • 0-7818-0097-8 • W • $8.95pb
• (288)

EGYPTIAN COOKING

Samia Abdennour

Almost 400 recipes, all adapted for the North American kitchen, represent the best of authentic Egyptian family cooking.

199 pages • 5½ x 8½ • 0-7818-0643-7 • NA • $11.95pb • (727)

ART OF SOUTH INDIAN COOKING

Alamelu Vairavan and Patricia Marquardt

Over 100 recipes for tempting appetizers, chutneys, rice dishes, vegetables and stews—flavored with onions, tomatoes, garlic, and delicate spices in varying combinations—have been adapted for the Western kitchen.

202 pages • 5½ x 8½ • 0-7818-0525-2 • W • $22.50 • (635)

BEST OF GOAN COOKING

Gilda Mendonsa

From Goa—a region in Western India once colonized by the Portuguese—comes a cuisine in which the hot, sour and spicy flavors mingle in delicate perfection, a reflection of the combination of Arabian, Portuguese and Indian cultures that have inhabited the region.

106 pages • 7 x 9¼ • 12 pages color illustrations • 0-7818-0584-8 • NA • $8.95pb • (682)

THE BEST OF KASHMIRI COOKING

Neerja Mattoo

With nearly 90 recipes and 12 pages of color photographs, this cookbook is a wonderful introduction to Kashmiri dishes, considered the height of gourmet Indian cuisine.

131 pages • 5½ x 8½ • 12 pages color photographs • 0-7818-0612-7 • NA • $9.95pb • (724)

THE ART OF PERSIAN COOKING

Forough Hekmat

This collection of 200 recipes features such traditional Persian dishes as Abgushte Adas • (Lentil soup), Mosamme Khoreshe • (Eggplant Stew), Lamb Kebab, Cucumber Borani • (Special Cucumber Salad), Sugar Halva and Gol Moraba • (Flower Preserves).

190 pages • 5½ x 8½ • 0-7818-0241-5 • W • $9.95pb • (125)

THE ART OF ISRAELI COOKING

Chef Aldo Nahoum

All of the 250 recipes are kosher.

"[Includes] a host of new indigenous Israeli recipes with dishes that reflect the eclectic and colorful nature of Israeli cuisine."—*Jewish Week*

125 pages • 5 x 8 • 0-7818-0096-X • W • $9.95pb • (252)

THE ART OF TURKISH COOKING
Nesret Eren

"Her recipes are utterly mouthwatering, and I cannot remember a time when a book so inspired me to take pot in hand."—Nika Hazelton, *The New York Times Book Review*

308 pages • 5 x 8 • 0-7818-0201-6 • W • $12.95pb • (162)

COOKING THE CARIBBEAN WAY
Mary Slater

Here are 450 authentic Caribbean recipes adapted for the North American kitchen, including Bermuda Steamed Mussels, Port Royal Lamb Stew, and Mango Ice-cream.

256 pages • 5½ x 8½ • 0-7818-0638-0 • W • $11.95pb • (725)

BAVARIAN COOKING
Olli Leeb

"*Bavarian Cooking* is what a good regional cookbook should be—a guide for those who wish to know the heart and soul of a region's cooking, a book that anchors its recipes in the culture that produced them, and a cookbook that brings delight to the casual reader as well as to the serious cook."—*German Life*

171 pages • 6½ x 8¼ • line illustrations and 10 pages color photographs • 0-7818-0561-9 • NA • $25.00hc • (659)

A BELGIAN COOKBOOK
Juliette Elkon

A celebration of the regional variations found in Belgian cuisine.

224 pages • 5½ x 8½ • 0-7818-0461-2 • W • $12.95pb • (535)

CELTIC COOKBOOK: Traditional Recipes from the Six Celtic Lands
Helen Smith-Twiddy

This collection of over 160 recipes from the Celtic world includes traditional, yet still popular dishes like *Rabbit Hoggan* and *Gwydd y Dolig* (Stuffed Goose in Red Wine).

200 pages • 5 x 8 • 0-7818-0579-1 • NA • $22.50hc • (679)

ENGLISH ROYAL COOKBOOK: FAVORITE COURT RECIPES
Elizabeth Craig

Dine like a King or Queen with this unique collection of over 350 favorite recipes of the English royals, spanning 500 years of feasts! Charmingly illustrated throughout.

187 pages • 5½ x 8½ • illustrations • 0-7818-0583-X • W • $11.95pb • (723)

TRADITIONAL RECIPES FROM OLD ENGLAND

Arranged by country, this charming classic features the favorite dishes and mealtime customs from across England, Scotland, Wales and Ireland.

110 pages • 5 x 8½ • illustrated • 0-7818-0489-2 • W • $9.95pb • (157)

THE ART OF IRISH COOKING

Monica Sheridan

Nearly 200 recipes for traditional Irish fare.

166 pages • 5 x 8 • illustrated • 0-7818-0454-X • W • $12.95pb • (335)

ART OF DUTCH COOKING

C. Countess van Limburg Stirum

This attractive volume of 200 recipes offers a complete cross section of Dutch home cooking, adapted to American kitchens. A whole chapter is devoted to the Dutch Christmas, with recipes for unique cookies and candies that are a traditional part of the festivities.

192 pages • 5 x 8 • illustrations • 0-7818-0582-1 • W • $11.95pb • (683)

TASTE OF MALTA

Claudia Caruana

Includes over 100 Maltese favorites like timpana (macaroni baked with tomatoes and ground meat enclosed in pastry), ross fil-forn (rice baked in meat sauce), and aljotta (fish soup with potatoes and garlic.)

250 pages • 5½ x 8½ • 0-7818-0524-4 • W • $24.95hc • (636)

MAYAN COOKING: CLASSIC RECIPES FROM THE SUN KINGDOMS OF MEXICO

Cherry Hamman

This unique cookbook contains not only 200 colorful and exotic recipes from the Mexican Yucatan, but also the author's fascinating observations on a vanishing way of life.

250 pages • 5½ x 8½ • 0-7818-0580-5 • W • $24.95hc • (680)

African Language Titles from Hippocrene . . .

BEMBA-ENGLISH/ENGLISH BEMBA COMPACT DICTIONARY

240 pages • 4 x 6 • 10,000 entries • 0-7818-0630-5 • $13.95pb • (709)

FULANI-ENGLISH PRACTICAL DICTIONARY

264 pages • 5 x 7¼ • 0-7818-0404-3 • $14.95pb • (38)

HAUSA-ENGLISH/ENGLISH-HAUSA
PRACTICAL DICTIONARY
431 pages • 5 x 7 • 18,000 entries • 0-7818-0426-4 • $16.95pb • (499)

LINGALA-ENGLISH/ENGLISH-LINGALA
DICTIONARY AND PHRASEBOOK
120 pages • 3¾ x 7 • 0-7818-0456-6 • $11.95pb • (296)

PULAAR-ENGLISH/ENGLISH-PULAAR
STANDARD DICTIONARY
275 pages • 5½ x 8¼ • 30,000 entries • 0-7818-0479-5 • $19.95pb • (600)

POPULAR NORTHERN SOTHO DICTIONARY:
SOTHO-ENGLISH/ENGLISH-SOTHO
335 pages • 4⅜ x 5⅜ • 25,000 entries • 0-627015-867 • $14.95pb • (64)

SOMALI-ENGLISH/ENGLISH-SOMALI
DICTIONARY AND PHRASEBOOK
176 pages • 3¾ x 7 • 1,400 entries • 0-7818-0621-6 • $13.95pb • (755)

SWAHILI PHRASEBOOK
184 pages • 4 x 5⅜ • 0-87052-970-6 • $8.95pb • (73)

BEGINNER'S SWAHILI
156 pages • 6¾ x 10 • 0-7818-0335-7 • $9.95pb • (52)

TWI BASIC COURSE
225 pages • 6½ x 8½ • 0-7818-0394-2 • $16.95pb • (65)

TWI-ENGLISH/ENGLISH-TWI CONCISE DICTIONARY
332 pages • 4 x 6 • 0-7818-0264-4 • $12.95pb • (290)

VENDA-ENGLISH DICTIONARY
490 pages • 6 x 8½ • 20,000 entries • 0-627-01625-1 • $39.95hc • (62)

YORUBA-ENGLISH/ENGLISH-YORUBA
CONCISE DICTIONARY
257 pages • 4 x 6 • 8,000 entries • 0-7818-0263-6- $14.95pb • (275)

ENGLISH-ZULU/ZULU-ENGLISH DICTIONARY
519 pages • 4¾ x 7¼ x • 30,000 entries • 0-7818-0255-5 • $29.50pb • (203)

Other African Interest Titles

TREASURY OF AFRICAN LOVE POEMS AND PROVERBS
A bilingual selection of songs and sayings from numerous African languages—including Swahili, Yoruba, Berber, Zulu and Amharic.
128 pages • 5 x 7 • 0-7818-0483-3 • $11.95hc • (611)

AFRICAN PROVERBS
This collection of 1,755 proverbs spans all regions of the African continent. They are arranged alphabetically by key words. Charmingly illustrated throughout.
135 pages • 6 x 9 • 20 illustrations • 0-7818-0691-7 • $17.50hc • (778)

NAMIBIA: THE INDEPENDENT TRAVELER'S GUIDE
313 pages • 5½ x 8½ • 26 maps, 22 illustrations, photos, index
• 0-7818-0254-7 • $16.95pb • (109)

All prices subject to change without prior notice. **To purchase Hippocrene Books** contact your local bookstore, call (718) 454-2366, or write to: HIPPOCRENE BOOKS, 171 Madison Avenue, New York, NY 10016. Please enclose check or money order, adding $5.00 shipping (UPS) for the first book and $.50 for each additional book.